THINGS to Make & Do FOR Advent & Christmas

Three more books will soon be available
in the Things to Make and Do series:

Things to Make and Do for Lent and Easter
Things to Make and Do for Pentecost
Things to Make and Do Anytime

THINGS to Make & Do FOR Advent & Christmas

Written and Compiled
by Martha Bettis Gee

Bridge Resources
Louisville, Kentucky

Book interior and cover design by Diane Cooke
Illustrations by Debora Weber

First Edition

Published by Bridge Resources
Louisville, Kentucky

http://www.bridgeresources.org

PRINTED IN THE UNITED STATES OF AMERICA
97 98 99 00 01 02 03 04 05 06 — 10 9 8 7 6 5 4 3 2 1

Library of Congress Cataloging-in-Publication Data

Gee, Martha Bettis, date.
    Things to make and do for Advent and Christmas / written and compiled by Martha Bettis Gee.
        p.   cm.
    Includes index.
    ISBN 1-57895-015-5
    1. Advent. 2. Christmas. 3. Bible crafts. 4. Christian education—Activity programs. 5. Creative activities and seat work.
    I. Title. II. Title: Things to make and do for Advent and Christmas.
    BV40. G44   1997
    268'.432—DC21   97–17816

Contents

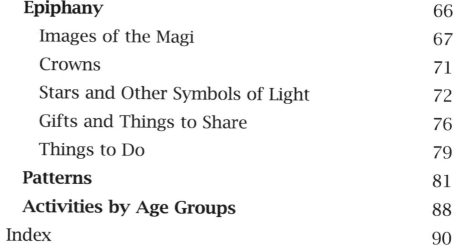

Introduction

The first of October signals the beginning of the winter holiday season. Displays of back-to-school clothing, pencils, and notebooks give way to Halloween candy and costumes. Merchants schedule sales before and after Thanksgiving as if the holiday were to celebrate what we buy, instead of a time to reflect and be thankful for what God has given us. But well before Thanksgiving, our streets and shopping malls have already become fantasy lands of glittering lights and Santa Clauses, all designed to encourage us to buy.

The church has its own story to tell. Advent signals the beginning of a time of preparation, reflection, and remembering that reaches a pinnacle in the joyous celebration of Jesus' birth at Christmas. Following Christmastide is the feast of the Epiphany, when the community of faith remembers the visit of the Magi from far away and reaffirms that Jesus, the Light of the world, came to all people.

Children need to hear and experience our faith story at all times of the year, but never more than at Christmas. Our culture tells them that spending money is the way to be happy and to show love, and it delivers this message by way of powerful sensory images—glittering lights, glowing colors, festive music, and savory smells. The story of the Word made flesh speaks powerfully of other truths. What better way to experience and express the yearnings and joys of the season than by engaging in creative activities that appeal to the senses?

About This Book

The activities in this book have been gathered from many places. Some were a part of curriculum resources over many years. Some are the fruit of twelve years' teaching experience and twenty-five years of working with children. Some came from the creative minds of colleagues and friends who love children. And some came from children themselves. Like all good creative activities, each one began as an idea that took shape in the hands of those who used it.

At the heart of the creative process is the working of the Spirit, moving and shaping and transforming the person engaged in the act of creation. Every activity suggested here awaits the unique approach that only you and your group of children can bring to it.

Using Creative Activities with Children

●●●●●●●●●●●●●●●●●●●●●●●●●●●

Creative activities . . .

- provide an avenue for God's Spirit to speak to children
- give children a vehicle for expressing ideas, concepts, and feelings
- express each person's uniqueness as a child of God, a creation unlike any other
- speak to the variety of gifts of the Spirit within the community of faith

Guidelines for Using These Activities

- Allow plenty of time for exploration and expression. Creative activities cannot be rushed!
- Give enough directions for children to create, but allow for variations and alternative uses of materials.
- Model good stewardship for children through the wise use of all resources. Many activities in this book use extra materials or scraps left over from previous activities. Help children understand that when they find creative uses for scraps of construction paper, they are being good stewards of our world. In the same way, help children learn to take good care of art materials. Securely closing the tops of glue bottles or paint containers and carefully putting away scissors and crayons ensure that these expensive art materials last as long as possible.
- Recognizing that every night one-fourth of the world's children go hungry, we do not recommend the use of food in art activities. One exception is the use of modeling dough and play dough made from flour and salt. We have not yet found a satisfactory substitute for these materials.

Young children can understand Advent, Christmastide, and Epiphany in these terms.

We get ready for Christmas during Advent:

- We prepare our homes.
- We make or buy presents for people we love.
- We light the candles on our Advent wreaths.
- We hear stories about Mary and Joseph and their trip to Bethlehem, about the angels' message to the shepherds, about the joy of Jesus' birth, and about the visit of the kings.
- We make special food or have special meals with our families.
- We think of ways to share what we have with others.
- We hear that God's love is for all people.

Younger elementary children build on those understandings.

- Long before the birth of Jesus, people hoped and longed for a Messiah.
- We prepare ourselves for the celebration of Jesus' birth by hearing stories of prophets and others who came before him and by hearing the wonderful story of Jesus' birth.
- We spend time in prayer and in thinking about what the coming of Jesus means to the world.
- We think about what it means to express God's love for all people.

Older elementary children add deeper understandings.

- People expected the Messiah to come and liberate them. They did not expect a humble baby born to poor parents who would grow up to save them from their sins.
- Our world prepares for Christmas by buying many material things. We prepare by reading what the prophets say about hope, peace, joy, and love. We find ways to live out those ideas by helping others.
- If Jesus came for all people of all cultures and times, Christians must find ways to express God's inclusive love.

ADVENT

. . . is a time for active waiting and preparing, a period for making our homes, our hearts, and our world ready for the coming of Christ at Christmas.

It is a time of *hope* . . .
thinking about what kind of world we hope for, and how we can help to bring it about.

It is a time to pray for *peace* . . .
thinking about those places in our homes, neighborhoods, and world where we so desperately need the Prince of Peace.

It is a time of *love* . . .
receiving expressions of love from others and demonstrating love ourselves.

It is a time of *joy* . . .
being with family and friends, finding concrete ways to make our joy real through music, dance, and creative activities.

4

Advent Wreaths
. . . .
A Traditional Wreath

Children of All Ages

Using an Advent wreath is a tangible way to mark the four weeks leading up to Christmas. Children can learn about the symbolism of the wreath as they make one together.

What You Need
- A wire wreath form
- Evergreen branches
- 5 candle holders
- 4 purple candles and 1 white candle (sometimes a pink candle is used for the fourth Sunday)
- Matches for lighting candles

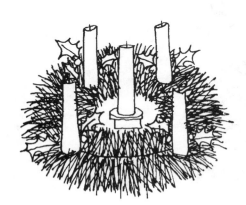

What You Do

1. Place the wreath form, the candles, and the candle holders on a low table and gather the children around it. Give each child some evergreen branches.

2. Begin a discussion about Advent wreaths by asking the children what season of the church year is just beginning. Children may respond that Christmas is coming. If they do, tell them that they are right, but the season just beginning is the time in the church year that Christians get ready for Christmas. It is called Advent.

3. Explain that the wreath is one way we mark the four Sundays until Christmas. Then ask the following questions: What shape is the wreath? (round, a circle) Can you find the beginning of the circle? (No, it is continuous.)

Tell them that the circle reminds us that God's love for us has no beginning and no end—it goes on forever.

4. Ask everyone to look at their evergreen branches. To begin a discussion about the symbolism of the evergreen, ask the following questions: What kind of tree did your branch come from? (Children may or may not know specific tree names such as cedar, pine, or spruce.)

Ask if this tree loses its leaves in winter. (No, it's an evergreen.)

Tell the children that the evergreen also reminds us of life everlasting. Invite each child to put his or her branch in the wreath. Don't be concerned about making the wreath neat right now, just let children put in the branches in whatever way they like.

5. Hold the candles and ask the following questions: How many candles are there? (four) Why do we use four candles? (one for each week until Christmas) What color are the candles? (purple)

Explain to the children that purple is a special color that reminds us of waiting. It helps us remember to take time to get ready for Jesus' coming. Tell the children that each candle reminds us of some important part of waiting and getting ready for Advent: The *first* candle is the prophecy candle, reminding us of hope. The *second* candle is the Bethlehem candle, reminding us of peace. The *third* candle is the shepherds' candle, reminding us to joyfully share the good news of Christ's coming. The *fourth* candle is the angels' candle, reminding us of God's love.

(Note: Adapt this to the traditions in your own congregation.)

What color is the fifth candle? (white)

Tell the children that this candle will be lit on Christmas Day. Invite individual children to put the four candles in the wreath and in the center.

6. When you have finished making the wreath, light the first candle and sing an Advent carol together.

7. Add branches to fill in the wreath after the activity is completed.

Grapevine Advent Wreaths

Older Elementary Children

This wreath uses the grapevine as a symbol for the quiet time of watching and waiting that characterizes Advent. The grapevine appears to be dead, but as spring arrives leaves erupt and in due time grapes ripen and are harvested. Let older children use a concordance to look up passages in the Bible that speak of the grapevine and the vineyard.

What You Need

- Grapevines or a purchased grapevine wreath
- Metal Advent wreath ring, or 4 candle holders
- An additional candle holder that will hold the white Christmas candle in the center of the wreath
- 4 purple candles and 1 white candle
- Wire cutters

What You Do

1. If you are using a purchased metal Advent wreath ring, show the children how to weave the grapevines in and out and around the ring until it is completely covered. At the end of one piece of vine, use the wire cutters to make a slanted cut. At the beginning of the next vine make another slanted cut so that the vines will lie flat when the ends are overlapped.

2. If you are using a purchased wreath, show the children how to separate the vines slightly so the four candle holders can be inserted around the edge of the wreath.

3. Put the candles in the candle holders.

4. Explain to the children that on Christmas Day they can place the white candle in the additional candle holder in the center of the wreath.

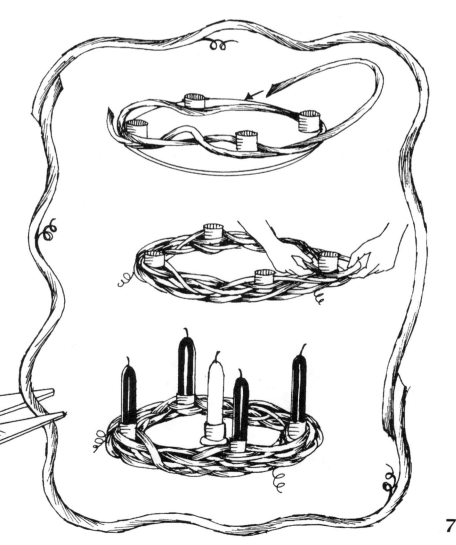

7

A Wreath of Hands

Younger Elementary Children

What You Need

- Green construction paper
- Scissors
- Purple construction paper for candles
- Large sheets of white construction paper or poster board
- Glue

What You Do

1. Tell children to trace their hands up to twenty times on green construction paper and cut them out.

2. On large sheets of construction paper, have each child glue the hands in the shape of a wreath.

3. Next ask the children to cut four purple candles to glue at intervals around the wreath.

✳ And More . . .

—*Make a Christmas wreath using the same method. Cut circles from red construction paper for berries and glue them on. Add a red construction-paper bow.*
—*Before gluing the hands on to form a wreath, the children could print on each one a "Christmas Good Deed" he or she plans to do, or individual ways to get ready for Christmas during Advent.*
—*Instead of using cut paper hands, have the children make handprints on white paper using green tempera paint mixed with a little liquid dishwashing soap.*

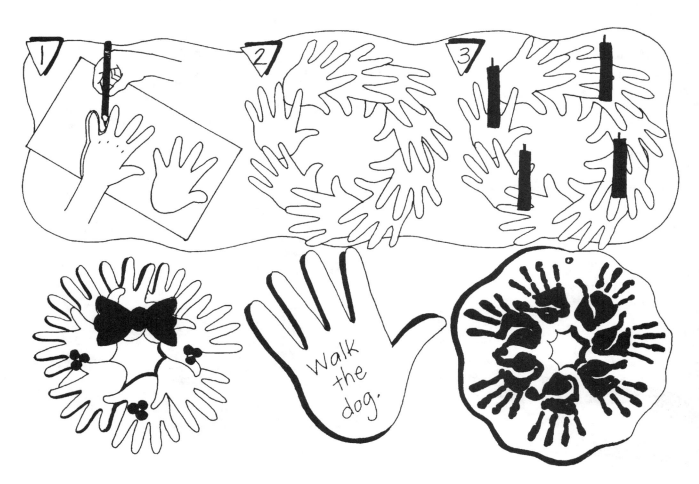

Miniature Advent Wreaths

Younger and Older Elementary Children

Children can make these tiny Advent wreaths to keep in their bedrooms during Advent.

What You Need

- Homemade play dough, tinted green

Ingredients:
- 1/2 cup salt
- 1 cup flour
- 2 tsp. cream of tartar
- 1 cup water
- 1 T vegetable oil
- Green food coloring

Mix together well. Over medium heat, stir constantly until mixture forms a ball. Let cool and knead until smooth. Store in an airtight container. Each recipe makes about 1 cup of dough (enough for 4–5 wreaths).

- Waxed paper
- Sheets of white paper with heavy black outline of a circle about 4" in diameter
- Birthday candles for each child (purple, if possible, or white)

What You Do

1. Give each child the paper with the circle outline and a sheet of waxed paper to lay on top of it.

2. Each child can roll the play dough into three thin "snakes." Show them how to join the three snakes at one end and braid the loose ends together. The completed braid should be at least one inch thick.

3. Children can use the circle outline under the waxed paper as a guide for forming the wreath shape from the braided play dough. They can join the ends together to make the circle complete.

4. Next, each child should insert four candles into the play dough wreath, spaced equidistant around the circle.

5. Set aside completed wreaths to air dry.

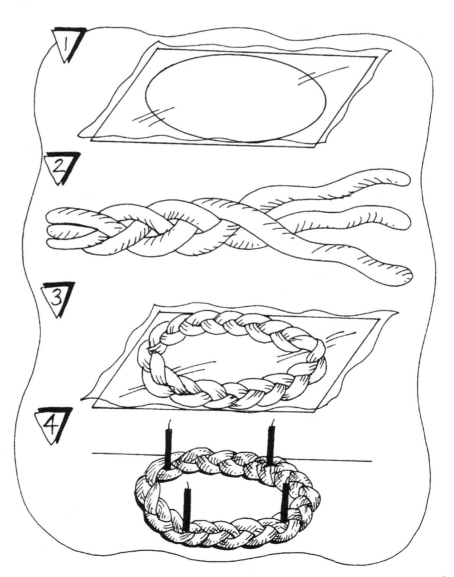

Advent Calendars and Other Ways of Marking Time

●●●●●●●●●●●

Christmas Card Advent Calendar

Younger and Older Elementary Children

What You Need

- 2 sheets of purple or blue construction paper
- Pictures from old Christmas cards, Christmas magazines, or old leaflet pictures from church school curriculum
- Scissors
- Glue
- Rulers
- Markers
- Masking tape

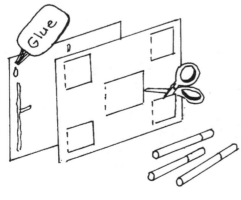

What You Do

1. Have children select four pictures approximately three by three inches and one nativity scene picture approximately three by four inches. Help the children visualize these sizes by cutting out samples or trimming index cards to these sizes.

2. Hand out two sheets of construction paper to each child. Show younger children how to fold the paper in fourths and make four doors in the four quadrants of the paper by measuring and marking three-inch squares. Older children can do this for themselves.

3. Have the children cut around three sides of each square, leaving the left side of each square uncut. Fold back to make doors.

4. Explain that they can use the same procedure to make a door in the center that is slightly larger, three by four inches.

5. Direct the children to lay the cut piece of construction paper on top of the uncut piece. Open each door and trace around the space where a picture should go so that it can be seen when the door is opened.

6. Have them remove the top sheet and glue the pictures to the bottom sheet.

7. Then tell them to close the doors and carefully glue the top sheet to the bottom sheet. Explain that they should be careful not to glue the doors shut.

8. On the center door, the children can print the word *Christmas.* Then they should label each of the other four doors with either *Hope, Peace, Love,* or *Joy.*

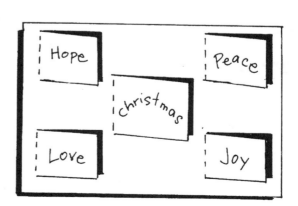

10

Giant Advent Calendar

Children of All Ages

This Advent calendar can be displayed on a bulletin board or in a hallway throughout the season of Advent. You will need the same number of pictures as there are days in the season of Advent. Check the calendar for the current year to see how many days are in the season. If you are working with a small group of children and have more days than you have children, invite another group to make the calendar with you, ask children to make more than one picture, or intersperse the children's pictures with sheets on which you have printed Bible verses selected from the lectionary passages for Advent.

What You Need

- Sheets of white drawing paper of varying sizes, from approximately 4 to 6 inches square
- 6-inch square sheets of blue or purple construction paper
- Butcher or mural paper
- Colored markers or crayons
- Heavy black marker
- Masking tape or staples to attach the calendar to the wall or bulletin board
- Clear tape
- Calendar
- Scissors

What You Do

1. Give each child a piece of drawing paper and tell the children to draw a picture that shows how we get ready for the coming of Jesus at Christmas during Advent.

2. With a heavy black marker, print the dates of the Advent season on individual construction-paper squares, beginning with the date of the First Sunday in Advent. Make a square for each date until December 25.

3. From butcher or mural paper, cut a large outline of a house by enlarging the pattern on p. 46. The outline should be approximately four feet wide by six feet high, but adjust the size to fit the space where it will be displayed. Tape or staple the outline in its display space.

4. Attach the completed children's pictures to the outline, leaving spaces between them so that they will resemble windows.

5. Use clear tape to attach the construction-paper squares in consecutive order over the pictures, taping the "shutters" over the pictures on one side only. If a shutter slips, use a small piece of masking tape to secure it closed.

6. Explain that every day one shutter can be removed to reveal the picture for that day, until all pictures are displayed on Christmas.

✸And More . . .

Paint a large appliance carton to make a giant apartment-house Advent calendar. Glue on red construction-paper bricks, or use markers to mark off bricks on the walls. Use one side of the box for each week of Advent. Make pictures and shutters as described in 4, 5, and 6 above.

Advent Kiosk Calendar

Younger and Older Elementary Children

A kiosk is made by stacking cartons to make a three-dimensional display. This Advent calendar can be an ongoing project in which one box is made each Sunday of Advent, or children can work in twos or threes to make the four boxes at once.

What You Need

- 4 sturdy cardboard cartons
- Purple and blue construction paper
- Blue tempera paint, brushes, and water (optional)
- Old magazines
- White glue
- Scissors

What You Do

1. Let the children cover each box with blue paper (or paint them in advance and set aside to dry).

2. From purple construction paper, cut out letters to spell *Hope, Peace, Joy,* and *Love.* Let the children glue a word to one side of each of the four cartons.

3. Have children cut out magazine pictures, phrases, or words that depict hope, peace, joy and love. They can use the other three sides of each carton to make a collage of pictures, phrases, or words about the word on that particular carton.

✳ And More . . .

Older elementary children could use a concordance and a list of Advent lectionary passages to find Bible verses that speak about the four key words. They can print the verses on the cartons.

Advent Tree Calendar

Older Elementary Children

Make an Advent calendar in the shape of a Christmas tree large enough to fit on the back of a door. Each day one message can be read, and on Christmas Day all the messages can be read in the order of the numbers on them. The Advent tree is a good gift idea for a person who cannot leave home.

What You Need

- Colored construction paper (red, blue, yellow)
- Patterns for ornaments found on p. 83 and tree pattern on p. 84
- Sheets of green paper or poster board for each calendar
- Scissors
- Pencils
- Glue
- Black fine-point markers
- Clear tape
- Cardboard for pattern templates
- Photocopies of messages for ornaments (see pp. 14–15)

What You Do

1. Enlarge the tree pattern on p. 84 according to the instructions. Make two or three templates from cardboard for the children to use.

2. Have each child trace around the tree template and cut out his or her tree.

3. Have the child cut twenty-four ornaments in several different shapes, using the patterns on p. 83. On one side, children can number the ornaments from one to twenty-four with the marking pens.

4. Photocopy the messages and cut them apart. Children can paste the messages on the other side of the ornaments.

5. Direct the children to attach the ornaments to the tree calendar with the tape, number side out.

Messages for Ornaments (to be photocopied)

1. This is the way
   Jesus Christ was born.

2. The angel said,
   "Mary, don't be
   afraid, for you'll
   have a baby."

3. "His name will be
   called Jesus, which
   means Savior."

4. Mary said,
   "My heart praises
   the Lord."

5. God is always
   saving the people.

6. God puts down the mighty
   from their thrones.

7. God lifts up those
   who feel unimportant.

8. God fills the hungry
   with good things.

9. God sends the
   rich away with
   empty hands.

10. God gives light
    to those in
    darkness.

11. God guides our
    feet into the path
    of peace.

12. The time came for
    Mary to have her baby.

13. She wrapped him in
    cloths and put him
    in a manger.

14. There were shepherds
    in that part of the country,
    and an angel appeared to
    them.

15. They were very frightened.

16. But the angel said
    to them, "Don't be
    afraid. I'm here with
    good news!"

17. "This very night your Savior was born, Jesus the Lord."

18. Suddenly a lot of angels appeared, singing praises.

19. "Glory to God in the highest!"

20. "Peace on earth to those with whom God is pleased."

21. The shepherds said, "Let's go to Bethlehem and see this thing that has happened."

22. They hurried and found Mary, Joseph, and the baby.

23. The shepherds went back singing praises to God for what they had heard and seen.

24. The child grew and became strong. He was full of wisdom, and God's blessings were with him.

"Peace on earth to those with whom God is pleased."

Advent Chain

Children of All Ages

What You Need

For each chain:

- 18 purple construction paper strips, 1" x 9", plus enough additional strips to represent each weekday between the last Sunday of Advent and Christmas. (This changes each year, so check the calendar.)
- 5 white or gold paper strips, 1" x 9"
- Tape or stapler

What You Do

1. Tell the children to tape together the ends of one white strip to make a ring. They should then put a strip of purple paper through the white ring and tape its ends to start the chain. They can add five additional purple rings, then one white or gold, then six purple, and so forth.

2. When the chains are completed, children can take them home to hang in their rooms. Tell them to take off one link of the chain every night until Christmas.

✳ And More . . .

—Older children can use fine-lined felt-tipped markers or pens to write a message inside each link before making the chain. They could use the messages suggested for the Advent Tree Calendar, or they could brainstorm together a list of small things they might do to prepare for Jesus' coming, such as "clean my room for Advent" or "babysit my sister so Mom can shop." Children could write something from the list on each link. Explain that when they remove a link, they should do whatever is written on it.

—Instead of gold or white paper for the four Sundays and Christmas, children might use metallic star garland for the links.

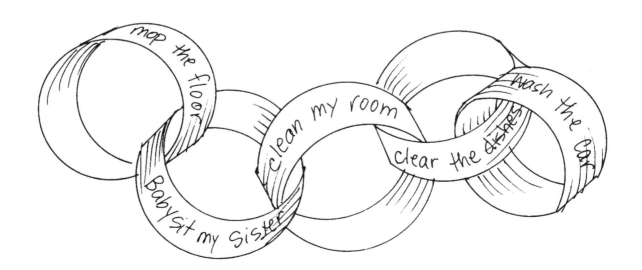

Advent Candle Ornaments

Younger Elementary Children

This simple ornament is a reminder of the four ideas we focus on during the four weeks of Advent.

What You Need

- A strip of purple or blue construction paper 2" x 12" for each child
- Scraps of yellow, orange, or red construction paper
- Fine-point marking pens
- White glue
- Ornament hangers

What You Do

1. Show children how to pleat the strip like a fan, beginning about one and a fourth inches from the top. They can make the rest of the pleats about the same size.

2. Tell the children to print the word *hope* on the second pleat, skip a pleat, and print *peace* on the next pleat. They can add the words *love* and *joy* in the same way.

3. From construction-paper scraps, have each child cut a flame shape and glue it to the top of the candle ornament. The ornament can be hung on the tree by carefully attaching a wire ornament hanger to the flame.

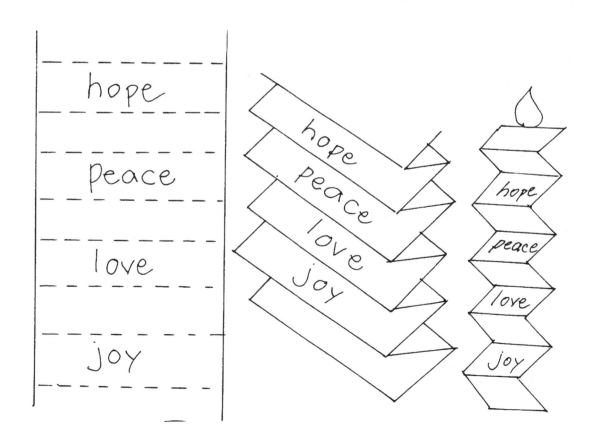

Activities for Remembering
● ● ● ● ● ● ● ● ● ● ●

The Jesse Tree and Other Remembering Symbols

Jesus is occasionally referred to in the Bible as coming from Jesse's tree or branch. Artists got the idea of using a tree as a symbol from Isa. 11:1. ("A shoot shall come out from the stump of Jesse, and a branch shall grow out of his roots.")

The artists made Jesse the stem or root, Mary the rod or shoot, and Christ the fruit. A Jesse Tree, window, or mobile is a way of remembering all those in the Old Testament who came before Jesus and who waited and longed for the coming of the Messiah.

Use the genealogy of Jesus found in Matt. 1:1–17 as a starting point, with the addition of the mothers not named in the list, such as Sarah and Rachel. You can also include Old Testament people such as Noah, who came before Abraham and Sarah. Expand the Jesse Tree idea to include others in the Bible who came after Jesus, like Lydia, and heroes in the Christian faith whose stories are part of the ongoing story of God's people.

Here is a list to get you started. It includes Old Testament people, Scripture references, and some suggested symbols. (See pp. 81–82 for patterns for the symbols.) The most effective Jesse Trees will use symbols the children choose to represent stories and characters they know.

Abraham	starry sky (Gen. 15:1–6)
Sarah	tent (Gen. 18:1–15)
Isaac	bundle of sticks (Gen. 22:1–19)
Rebekah	water jar (Gen. 24)
Jacob	ladder (Gen. 28:10–15)
Joseph	coat of many colors (Gen.37:2–11)
Moses	stone tablets (Ex. 24:12–18)
Miriam	tambourine (Ex. 15:20–21)
Gideon	sword or trumpet (Judg. 7)
Ruth	sheaf of grain (Ruth 2:1–15)
David	lyre (1 Sam. 16:14–22)
Jeremiah	yoke (Jer. 28)

Stained-Glass Jesse Tree Window

Older Elementary Children

A stained-glass window in the Chartres Cathedral in France portrays the Jesse Tree. Made hundreds of years ago in the year 1150, it is one of the earliest examples of a beautiful window showing the family tree of Jesus. This tree was one of the most popular subjects for stained-glass windows in the early cathedrals. It helped people who could not read to trace the ancestry of Jesus back to Jesse, the father of David.

What You Need

- A large sheet of cardboard or the side of an appliance box
- Pencil
- Bible
- Sheets of clear acetate
- Colored transparency pens
- X-Acto knife
- Clear tape
- Ruler
- Clean rag

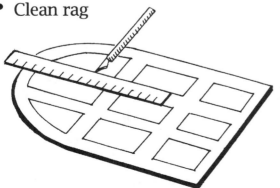

What You Do

1. In advance, prepare the window frame. Using the pattern below as a guide, draw with a pencil the design of the window, with openings large enough for the separate drawings. Include a space in the center of a round window or at the top of a long narrow window for the drawing of Mary, Joseph, and Jesus. Make sure that the framing around each opening is at least an inch wide so that the whole window will remain sturdy as you work on it. Use the X-Acto knife to cut the openings yourself.

2. Let the children choose familiar names from Jesus' family tree in Matt. 1:1–17 as well as other biblical characters whose stories they know.

3. Let the children decide who will draw each character. Be sure to include a drawing of Mary, Joseph, and Jesus.

4. Have the children use the transparency pens to draw pictures of the characters on the sheets of acetate. Print at the bottom of each picture the name of the person in the picture. (Washable transparency ink can be wiped off if children wish to change their work or correct mistakes.)

5. Fasten the completed pictures to the back of the frame with clear tape. If you wish, make small openings along the bottom part of the frame so that each artist may make a small acetate design to show who did the work. It might be as portrait, a coat of arms, a monogram, or a signature.

6. When the window is complete, place it where light can shine through it.

Mary, Joseph + Jesus

Jesse Tree

Younger and Older Elementary Children

What You Need

- Patterns of suggested symbols from pp. 81–82 and list of biblical characters, Scripture references, and suggested symbols (see p. 18)
- Bibles
- White construction paper or other heavy drawing paper
- Felt-tipped pens or crayons
- Felt or poster board
- White glue
- Tree branch
- 5-pound coffee can
- Plaster of paris and water; container for mixing
- Scissors
- Paper punch
- Yarn or ornament hangers

What You Do

1. In advance, make the tree, or allow time for older elementary children to do so with supervision. Mix the plaster of paris and water according to the directions on the package. Pour carefully into the coffee can, filling it about halfway. Allow to partially set. Insert the tree branch into the can, and carefully fill the can until it is about three-quarters full. Hold the branch steady until the plaster of paris is set.

2. Discuss with the children what people of the faith they would like to include on their Jesse Tree. Encourage children to choose their own symbols for characters if they like.

3. Let the children decide who will make each symbol.

4. Distribute markers or crayons and heavy drawing paper so each child can draw a symbol.

5. When the symbols are finished, have the children cut them out and glue them to poster board or felt backing to make them sturdier.

6. Next, children can decorate the Jesse Tree with the symbols they have made. Attach by punching a small hole in the top of each symbol and tying on the branch with yarn; or use Christmas tree ornament hangers.

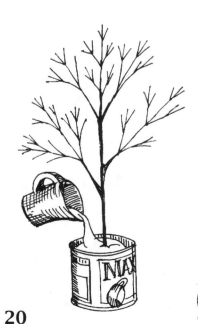

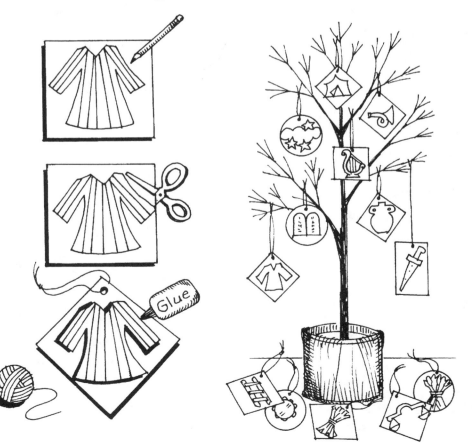

20

Jesse Tree Mobile

Younger and Older Elementary Children

Instead of displaying the symbols on a tree branch anchored in a can, make a mobile.

What You Need

- Patterns of suggested symbols from pp. 81–82 and list of biblical characters, Scripture references, and suggested symbols (see p. 18)
- Bibles
- White construction paper or other heavy drawing paper
- Felt-tipped pens or crayons
- Felt or poster board
- White glue
- Tree branch
- Lightweight monofilament fishing line
- Scissors

What You Do

1. In advance, determine where the mobile will be hung. Locate the central point of the tree branch and use monofilament fishing line to hang it.

2. Have the children make symbols as described in the Jesse Tree activity.

3. Hang the symbols from the tree branch with monofilament line. You will need to work carefully to balance the mobile so that it is even.

Foil Jesse Tree Ornaments

Older Elementary Children

What You Need

- Squares of aluminum foil, approximately 3 1/2" to 4" square
- Permanent felt-tipped markers
- String or yarn
- White glue
- Poster board or cardboard cut into 3-inch squares
- Paper punch
- Tape
- Felt cut into 3-inch squares (optional)
- Symbol patterns (pp. 81–82)
- Ruler
- Scissors
- Pencils

What You Do

1. Have the children choose one of the Jesse Tree symbol patterns from pp. 81–82, or invite them to think of a biblical character and a symbol to represent the person. They can sketch lightly or trace the symbol onto the cardboard square.

2. Tell the children to go over the outline of the symbol with a thin line of glue, press a length of string or yarn into the glue, and let dry.

3. When the glue is completely dry, tell the children to place a piece of foil over the cardboard and to press the foil onto the cardboard, running a finger over both sides of the string to make a raised design. They then fold the extra foil to the back of the cardboard and tape it down to secure it.

4. Children can use permanent felt-tipped markers to color in the design. Bright colors work best.

5. Glue a felt square to the back of the ornament, or glue two ornaments back-to-back to make a two-sided ornament.

6. Punch a hole in the top of the ornament and add string for hanging.

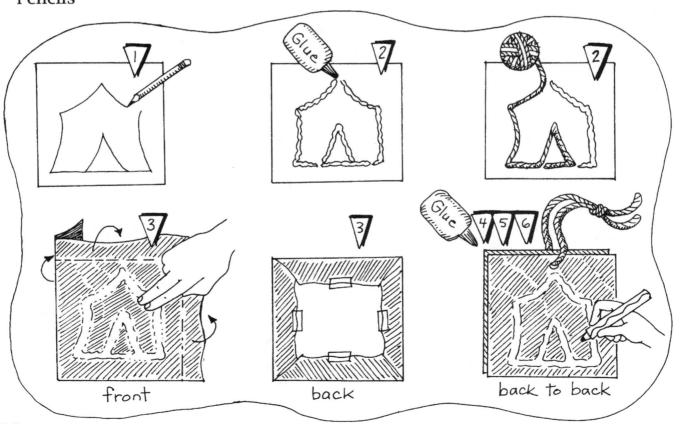

front

back

back to back

Memory Strips

Younger and Older Elementary Children

Making a memory strip creates a picture that will remind the child who made it of a series of stories or events like prophecies about Advent; Old Testament characters who came in the long years before Jesus; or the events in the Christmas narrative.

What You Need

- Burlap, felt or heavy paper strips one yard long and 6" wide (one per child)
- Felt, yarn, and construction-paper scraps
- Pins, glue, masking tape
- Scissors
- Marking pens

What You Do

1. Tell children to think of a picture that will help them remember the story or event and use the art supplies to make a picture.

2. Glue or pin each child's picture to the memory strip.

3. When the memory strip is complete, children can take turns telling each other the stories.

23

Advent Story Strip

Younger Elementary Children

What You Need

- Colored construction paper (8 1/2" x 11")
- White butcher or shelf paper
- Crayons or colored markers
- Scissors
- Ruler

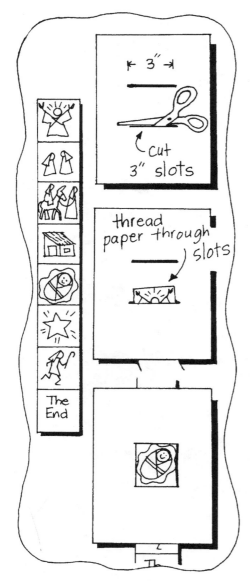

What You Do

1. Cut the butcher or shelf paper into strips about twenty-four by three inches. Mark the strips into three-inch squares.

2. Help the children recall the events leading up to Jesus' birth. You might include the angel appearing to Mary, Mary visiting Elizabeth, the journey to Bethlehem, finding no room at the inn, and so forth.

3. Direct the children to draw the scenes from the story, one scene in each square, leaving the first square blank.

4. When they have finished, help them draw a three-inch square in the middle of a sheet of colored paper, using a ruler or tracing around a cardboard square. Show the children how to turn the paper sideways and cut along the two opposite sides of the square.

5. The story strip may now be threaded through the square from behind. As it is pulled through the opening, it will reveal one scene from the story at a time.

6. Cut off any of the strip that was not used, with the exception of one blank square at the end of the story. In this square write "THE END." The title of the story may be written above the square on the colored paper.

7. Encourage each child to tell the story in his or her own words as the scenes are pulled through the square.

✳And More . . .

Make a giant story strip from strong shelf paper or butcher paper about twelve inches wide and marked off in twelve-inch squares. The length will depend on the number of children working on the story. Cut the sides only of a twelve-inch square in the center of a sheet of poster board through which to run the strip. Hang the poster board frame with clothespins or strong spring clips from a chart track, clothes rack, or a piece of clothesline stretched between two heavy chairs. Let each child choose one event to illustrate in a square.

Concepts and Images

• • • • • • • • • • •

Picturing Peace

Older Elementary Children

After seeing Edward Hicks's painting *The Peaceable Kingdom,* children can illustrate words from Isaiah that describe the kinds of things they want most to happen in the realm in which the Messiah rules.

What You Need
- A print of Edward Hicks's *The Peaceable Kingdom*
- Bibles
- Sheets of white drawing paper or poster board
- Old magazines
- Scissors
- White glue, slightly diluted with water
- Brushes

What You Do

1. Show the children the print of *The Peaceable Kingdom.* Ask someone to read aloud Isa. 11:1-9. Say, "Edward Hicks was an American Quaker preacher who especially loved this Bible passage. He used it as the subject of many paintings. This is one of them." Ask the children to tell you what they see. What kind of animals are together. Would a lion really be close to a lamb without trying to kill it? Could a small child lie down with a wild animal? What is the artist trying to say? Then say: "Think of a scene about peacemaking today that you could include in your picture. Would you like to see an end to atomic weapons, strikes, hunger, or mistreatment of the poor? How could you show your special concern in your picture? What kinds of people or groups who are enemies could you show together in your picture? What words or phrases would make your idea about peacemaking clear?"

2. Let the children choose pictures, words, or phrases from the magazines to make a collage on the paper. Show them how to position the picture or phrase on the paper, then paint *over* it with the diluted white glue. Children may need you to show how pictures and phrases can be overlapped slightly to cover the whole page.

3. Allow pictures to dry completely.

4. Display the completed pictures with the Edward Hicks print.

Road Signs for Advent

Older Elementary Children

What You Need

- Bibles
- Highway road test booklet (illustration of road signs)
- Purple or blue poster board or construction paper
- Felt-tipped markers
- Thin dowels or other sticks for signs
- Tape
- Newsprint

What You Do

1. Have the children look up and read aloud Isa. 40:3–5 and Mark 1:2–4. Tell them that it was customary in the ancient world to prepare a processional path along which the image of a deity would be carried in the annual religious festival. It might be a wide, level pathway from which obstacles had been cleared.

2. To begin a discussion about Advent, ask the children, "What can we do to prepare the way for the coming of Jesus at Christmas?"

3. Have the children identify the road signs in the road test booklet. What kinds of messages are on the signs?

4. Relate the road signs to the season of Advent by asking the following questions: What should we stop during Advent in order to get ready? Of what should we be cautious? To what should we yield? Print the children's responses on newsprint.

5. Give the children purple or blue paper and tell them to make a road sign for Advent. Tape thin dowels to the back of the signs.

✴ And More . . .

When children have completed the signs, work together to make a poster for each sign that tells one or two things people can do to "obey" the sign. For example, if a sign says STOP BUYING SO MUCH, children might give one or two suggestions for gifts of service. Set the road signs up along a hallway with the accompanying posters next to them.

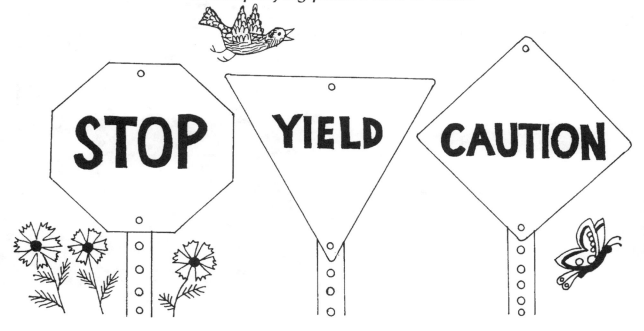

Prophet Messages

Older Elementary Children

What You Need

- Bibles
- Index cards with the following Scriptures: Isa. 9:2; 11:1–5; 11:6–7; 40:3–4; Jer. 31:33–34; Micah 4:2–4
- Posters with the names of the prophets (Isaiah, Jeremiah, Micah)
- Drawing paper
- Markers or crayons
- White glue or glue sticks

What You Do

1. Let each child choose a Scripture card and read it.

2. Ask each child to draw a picture of the image the prophet is using to tell about the time when the Messiah will come.

3. When the pictures are finished, ask the children to glue their pictures to the appropriate poster.

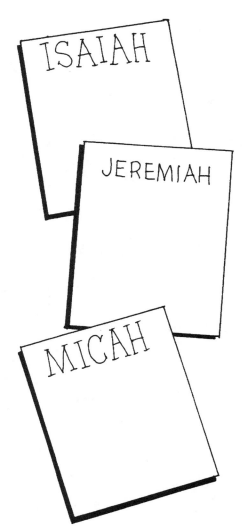

Things to Do

Time Tunnel

Older Elementary Children

The time tunnel journey helps children visualize the many hundreds of years that people waited and longed for the coming of the Messiah and how long ago the events occurred.

What You Need

- 100 feet of string
- Clear tape
- Index cards
- Markers
- Tape measure

What You Do

1. Make individual index cards for each of the following:

The present	The American Revolution
You are born.	Birth of Jesus
Your parents are born.	Abraham and Sarah
Abraham Lincoln is president.	Ruth and Boaz
	David

(If you like, make other cards with Old Testament characters or other names from the genealogy of Jesus found in Matthew 1.)

2. One foot will represent about forty years; an inch is a little over three years. Find the center of the string, which will represent the birth of Jesus. Tape that card to the center.

3. At one end of the string, tape the card for the present time. Moving back toward the middle tape marker, attach the following cards:

You are born—about two inches farther along

Your parents are born—about nine inches

Abraham Lincoln is president—three feet

The American Revolution—approximately four feet

4. Midway between the birth of Christ and the other end of the string, put the card to mark the story of Abraham and Sarah. Moving back toward the Birth of Jesus card, attach the following names:

Ruth and Boaz   David

The end of the string could represent the beginning of the world.

5. To use the string as a time tunnel, wind it through a number of rooms, through a hallway, a stairway, or outdoors. The more places the string can go the more fun it will be. Hold on to the string and follow it all the way to the end.

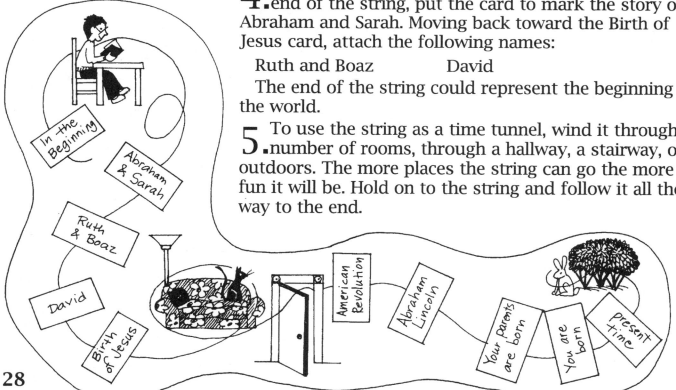

28

Be a Candle
Young Children

What You Do

1. Tell the children that they are going to be candles. "Light" the candles by having them cup their hands over their heads to make flames. With your own hands cupped over your head, lead them around the room, walking slowly.

2. Say, "Oh, I can feel a breeze! What do you think our candle flames will do?" (*Move*) Move your cupped hands back and forth, directing them to do the same.

3. Lead them around until you are standing in a circle. Then say, "The wax is melting, and the hot wax is running down the sides of our candles." Have them move their hands slowly down the sides of their bodies. Then say, "Our candles are burning down," and have them follow you as you sink slowly to your knees.

4. Walk around the circle and "blow" each candle out.

Advent Rings
Young Children

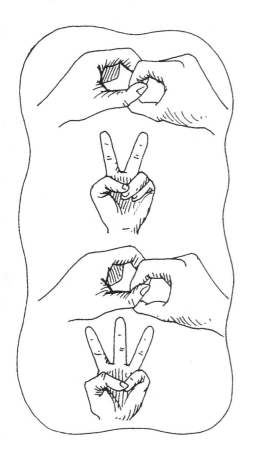

What You Do

1. Use the following as a fingerplay with the children:

> Here's a ring,
>> (*form circle with thumb and forefinger*)
>
> And here's a ring,
>> (*link thumb and forefinger of other hand through the first*)
>
> And one more ring makes three.
>> (*hold up three fingers*)
>
> Another ring, another ring,
>> (*link fingers as before*)
>
> And two more rings I see.
>> (*hold up two fingers*)
>
> We count the Advent rings, one by one,
>> (*count off fingers*)
>
> And wait for Christmas Day to come.

2. Use the fingerplay as you and the children remove rings from the Advent chain. Count off the rings on the chain as you say the words, and let individual children remove them. Then count the separate rings once again as you repeat the last two lines.

29

Straw for the Manger

Younger Elementary Children

What You Need

- Shoebox painted brown
- Small doll wrapped in a blanket (should fit in the shoe box)
- Yellow construction paper (12" x 18") cut into 1-inch strips (1 sheet per child)

What You Do

1. Give each child a stack of construction-paper strips. Show them the manger you made from the shoe box and the doll that will represent the baby Jesus.

2. Tell the children that as a group you are going to try to fill Jesus' manger with straw before Christmas. Tell them that every time they do something special for someone else, such as wash the dishes for their parents or help a friend with homework, they can print the good deed on a strip of "straw" and put it in the manger.

3. Try to fill the manger full of straw for Jesus' bed.

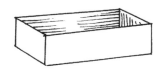

Let's Get Ready

Young Children

Use this simple chant to help children understand Advent as a time of preparation for Christmas.

What You Need

- Simple rhythm instruments

What You Do

1. Say the chant once, then have the children repeat it after you:

(*put emphasis on the highlighted syllables*)

(*clap*) (*clap*) (*clap*)   (*clap*) (*clap*) (*clap*)
Let's get ready,   **Let's get rea**dy
(*clap*)   (*clap*) (*clap*)   (*clap*) (*clap*)
Soon it will be **time** for **Christ**mas **to come!**

2. Then try starting at a faint whisper and clapping very softly. Repeat it several times, each time getting louder and louder.

3. Add simple rhythm instruments as you use the chant.

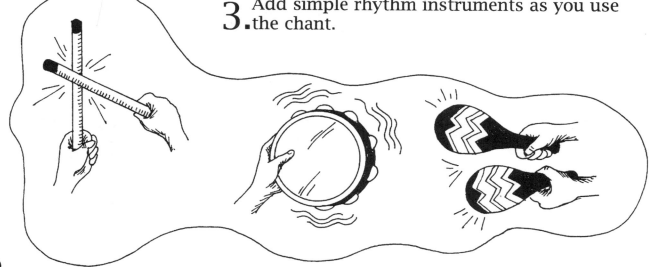

Waiting
Younger Elementary Children

What You Do

1. Say this poem:

The people were waiting, waiting, waiting,
   When would it be time?
"How long," they cried, "will we have to wait?"
   "When will it be time?"

The people were waiting, waiting, waiting,
   When would it be time?
"God has promised to send us a Savior
   When will it be time?"

The people were waiting, waiting, waiting,
   It was almost time!
The people were waiting, waiting, waiting,
   It was almost time!
The people were waiting, waiting, waiting,
   It was almost time!

2. Instead of saying "the people" in the first verse, substitute the names of Old Testament prophets like Isaiah or Jeremiah.

Poem is by Mary Kaye Fisher, adapted from *Children at Home,* winter 1987–88. Copyright 1987, The Geneva Press.

Jeremiah

Isaiah

CHRISTMASTIDE

A period of twelve days beginning with Christmas Day, Christmastide is the joyous culmination of the reflection and waiting that characterized Advent.
    We celebrate . . .

The One True Light . . .

Employing candlelight and lighted trees to symbolize the light that shines in darkness, and shining that light on the dark places of our world.

The Incarnation . . .

Demonstrating through acts of love and giving what it means for the Word to be made flesh.

Emmanuel, God-With-Us . . .

Identifying with the broken world and ministering to it even as we recognize our own brokenness.

Our Redeemer . . .

Reflecting and praying about the ultimate fulfillment of God's saving purpose and its beginning in the birth of Jesus.

Christmas Cards

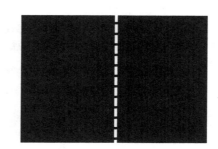 

Use sheets of 8 1/2" x 11" colored construction paper folded in the middle for each Christmas card.

Sponge Print Cards

Younger and Older Elementary Children

What You Need

- Clean sponges
- Patterns from p. 83
- Scissors
- Folded construction paper
- Tempera paint in Christmas colors (dilute with a little liquid dishwashing soap)
- Aluminum pie pans or shallow dishes for paint

What You Do

1. Cut clean dry sponges into Christmas shapes using the patterns.

2. Pour one color of tempera paint into each aluminum pie pan or shallow dish.

3. The child can dip the sponge shape into tempera paint, and carefully print on the front side of the folded construction-paper card.

4. Set aside to dry.

5. Children can add a Christmas message on the inside of the card.

Greetings by the Yard

Younger Elementary Children

What You Need for Each Card

- A piece of white adding machine tape 36" long
- Old magazines or Christmas cards
- Scissors
- White glue

What You Do

1. Have children decide on the message they want to communicate. You can say a lot on this card.

2. Have each child accordion fold the adding machine tape every four inches so it will fit into an envelope.

3. Pass out old magazines or Christmas cards so children can look for words and pictures that communicate their message.

4. Ask them to glue these all along the paper from one end to the other. Allow to dry before putting into envelopes.

Puffy Cards

Younger or Older Elementary Children

What You Need

- Facial tissue, green tissue paper, foil
- Pencil
- White glue
- Patterns from p. 83
- Felt-tipped markers
- Construction paper

What You Do

1. Cut lots of half-inch squares of the paper you have chosen to use.

2. Hold up the patterns and have the children decide what kind of picture they want to do (Christmas tree, star).

3. Each child can lightly draw the desired design on the front of the card using the patterns on p. 83 or their own ideas.

4. Have them place the eraser end of a pencil in the middle of each square and fold it up around the pencil. Then they dip the tip of the covered end of the pencil into glue.

5. Children then press the square into place on the construction-paper card inside the outline of the pattern. They do this over and over until every bit of the design is covered. They can add details with the markers.

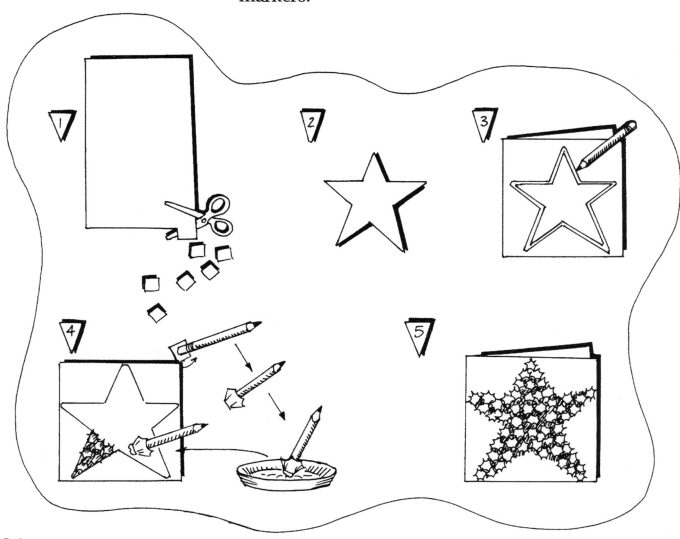

String Print Cards

Young Children and Younger Elementary Children

What You Need

- String
- Tempera paint in Christmas colors
- Aluminum pie pans or shallow dishes
- Books for weight (cover with foil to protect from paint)
- Folded construction paper for cards
- Markers

What You Do

1. Pour one color of tempera paint into each aluminum pie pan or shallow dish.

2. Direct the children to lay the folded construction paper cards on the table.

3. They then dip a piece of string in paint of a contrasting color.

4. Have them position the wet string on the card in a twisted swirl with one end sticking over the edge and put another piece of paper on top of the wet string.

5. Tell them to place a book over the paper for weight. Now they pull the wet string out slowly. The string will make an interesting design on the card.

6. Allow to dry.

7. Children can print a word of greeting over the design and write a message inside.

Giant Christmas Card

Children of All Ages

Four groups of children can work on this card. Put it in an area where members of the church can see and enjoy it.

What You Need

- Large appliance box
- Red or green tempera paint, brushes, painting smocks, water
- 4 pieces of heavy white butcher or mural paper cut slightly smaller than the sides of the box
- Construction paper and wrapping paper scraps
- Glue or masking tape
- Colored markers

What You Do

1. Paint the entire outside of the box. (Young children really enjoy doing this!) Let dry thoroughly.

2. Give each group of children a large piece of paper and the other art materials. Tell them to make a Christmas card for one side of the box. Ask them to be sure to leave white space where they can sign their names to the card.

3. When the groups are done, use white glue or masking tape to attach the cards to the sides of the box. Let children sign and add their own special greetings to the entire congregation.

Christmas Bookmark Greetings

Younger and Older Elementary Children

Here's a Christmas greeting and a gift rolled into one.

What You Need

- Clear adhesive plastic
- Scraps of Christmas greens, sequins, glitter
- Scissors
- Yarn or ribbon
- Construction-paper tags (red or green paper cut approximately 1" x 2")
- Fine-lined markers or pens
- Paper punch

What You Do

1. Have the children cut two strips of clear adhesive plastic the size they want the bookmark to be.

2. Show them how to carefully peel the backing off one piece.

3. On the sticky side of the plastic, tell them to arrange some scraps of Christmas greens, a few sequins, and some glitter. When the design is done, the children can take the backing off the other piece of plastic and place it on top.

4. Children can punch a hole in one end of the bookmark and run a small piece of yarn or ribbon through it. Knot to hold in place.

5. Children can attach a construction-paper tag to the ribbon on which they have printed a Christmas greeting.

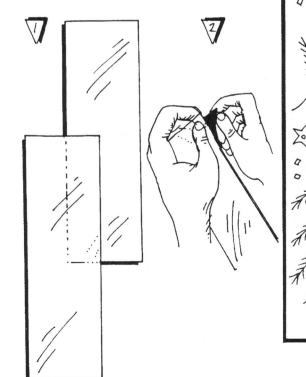

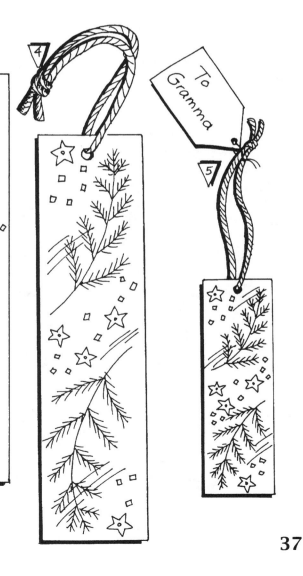

37

Other Messages

A Birth Announcement for Jesus

Younger Elementary Children

What You Need

- Red or green construction paper (8 1/2" x 11")
- Sheets of white paper slightly smaller, about 7 1/2" x 10"
- Markers
- White glue
- Old Christmas cards
- Scissors

What You Do

1. Glue a piece of white paper to a sheet of colored construction paper (the white paper should be slightly smaller).

2. Fold the paper in half so that the white sheet is on the outside forming a colored border. Fold again so that there are four sides to the card.

3. On the inside, children can print a message such as this:

   Mary and Joseph want you to know
   The baby has come!
   It's a boy!
   His name is Jesus—Emmanuel
   God is with us.

4. On the front of the card they can print "Good News to Everyone" or "Joy to All People."

5. Children can finish the card by decorating with cutouts from old Christmas cards or small drawings.

Sandwich Boards

Younger Elementary Children

Children can design and wear a sandwich board that shows in words and pictures some of the feelings the shepherds might have had when they found Jesus.

What You Need

- Corrugated cardboard box for each child, or 2 sheets of heavy poster board
- Yarn
- Markers or crayons
- Hole punch, X-Acto knife or carton cutter

What You Do

1. In advance, make sandwich boards by cutting out two sides of a large corrugated cardboard box with an X-Acto knife, or provide two sheets of heavy poster board for each child.

2. Talk with the children about what the shepherds might have said to one another when they first saw the baby Jesus. Would they have been surprised? amazed? overcome with joy? Have each child print in large letters what he or she thinks a shepherd might have said. Children should put the messages on both sheets of cardboard.

3. Have each child decorate with pictures or designs that illustrate the words.

4. Punch holes at the top edge of each board and connect the two boards with lengths of yarn. Slip it over the child's head.

5. Have a parade through the hallways with children wearing their sandwich boards.

✶ And More . . .

—*Use the same procedure to make sandwich boards for the Wise Men.*

—*Instead of putting words on the front of the sandwich board, have children use fabric, markers, yarn, and other materials to make a shepherd. Use the back of the sandwich board for the words the shepherd might have said.*

Collage Banners

Young Children and Younger Elementary Children

What You Need

- Sheet of butcher paper (cut to fit the space in which it will be displayed)
- Markers
- Red, green, gold, and silver paper scraps (construction paper, used gift wrap, wallpaper samples, and so forth)
- White glue
- Pencil

What You Do

1. In advance, use a pencil to draw large outline letters of a Christmas word like Joy or Alleluia on the butcher paper. Let the word completely fill the space. Go over the pencil with a marker.

2. Tell the children to tear the paper into small pieces and glue it onto the outlined letters, covering them completely. Encourage them to combine colors and textures of paper.

3. When the glue is dry, display the banner.

Drop Banner

Older Elementary Children

Making a drop banner is a project your group can use to announce the birth of Jesus to others in the church.

What You Need

- Bibles
- Pieces of lightweight cardboard or poster board in varying sizes of squares and rectangles
- Yarn scraps
- A paper punch and scissors
- Markers or crayons
- A long stick for hanging the banner (curtain rod, dowel, or yardstick)

What You Do

1. Tell the children to think of as many ways as they can to declare, announce, or tell about the birth of Jesus. Tell them to use words, phrases, and pictures from the Bible and from stories they have read or heard. If the finished banner will be hung on a wall, decorate only one side of the cardboard pieces. If it will be in an open space, have them illustrate both sides.

2. Have each child choose a piece of poster board that will fit what he or she is going to portray. For example, a square piece would work well for drawing a manger scene, while a long narrow rectangle might be best for printing and decorating the word "Halleluia!"

3. When children have completed their pieces, make the banner by punching holes in the tops of the pieces and attaching pieces to one another with brightly colored yarn.

4. Attach to the hanging stick with yarn.

✱ And More . . .

—*Make a hanging banner of the Luke 2 Christmas narrative. Divide the passage into sections. Print the sections on individual pieces of poster board. Have the children each choose a section to illustrate. Put the banner together in sequence using the instructions above.*
—*Illustrate a favorite Christmas carol or Advent hymn.*

Name Mobile

Young Elementary Children

This mobile helps children understand the meaning of Jesus' name.

What You Need

- Rectangular pieces of poster board (approximately 4" x 12")
- Colored construction paper cut into different shapes (circles, squares, diamonds, ovals)
- String or yarn cut in different lengths
- Colored markers
- Scissors
- Paper punch

What You Do

1. Print the name "Jesus" in large letters on the poster board rectangle.

2. Punch five holes along the bottom edge of the poster board. Punch two holes near the center of the top edge.

3. On five differently shaped pieces of construction paper, children can print the meaning of Jesus' name, one word per shape: "He will help his people."

4. Punch a hole at the top of each shape.

5. Children can tie the shapes to the poster board rectangle in order, using the shortest yarn for the first word and increasingly longer pieces for the subsequent words.

6. Thread yarn through the top two holes in the rectangle for hanging the mobile.

✳ And More . . .

Make a name mobile using the name Emmanuel and its meaning "God with us." Or use "Messiah" and the descriptive phrases from Isaiah: "Wonderful Counselor, Mighty God, Everlasting Father, Prince of Peace."

Tissue Paper Banners

Older Elementary Children

These banners are striking when hung in a sunny window. Use plenty of color to make them most effective. *Note: Children really enjoy spritzing the food coloring. Caution them not to overdo it.* (Another whole project might be to lay sheets of white tissue paper on the floor and allow children to spritz the coloring to their hearts' content, then use the sheets for wrapping paper.)

What You Need

- Drawing paper and pencils
- Sheets of white tissue paper
- Spritzer bottles with diluted food coloring (for Advent, purple and blue; for Christmas, red and green)
- Colored tissue paper
- Glue sticks
- Scissors
- Thin dowel stick or other sticks for hanging

What You Do

1. Have each child decide on a design for a banner and sketch it on a piece of plain drawing paper.

2. Show children how to spritz the sheet of white tissue paper with a light coat of food coloring. Allow to dry.

3. From colored tissue paper, children can cut and arrange the pieces for the banner on a piece of background tissue paper. Some shapes may be slightly overlapped, but be sure that the colors will still be evident when the light shines through the banner.

4. When they are satisfied with their design, children can glue the shapes to the background with the glue stick.

5. Fold over about an inch at the top of the banner and tape or glue down. Insert dowel stick for hanging.

6. Add a fringed border to the bottom of the banner, if desired.

✷And More . . .

Children who are not adept at using scissors can make banners by tearing shapes from the tissue paper.

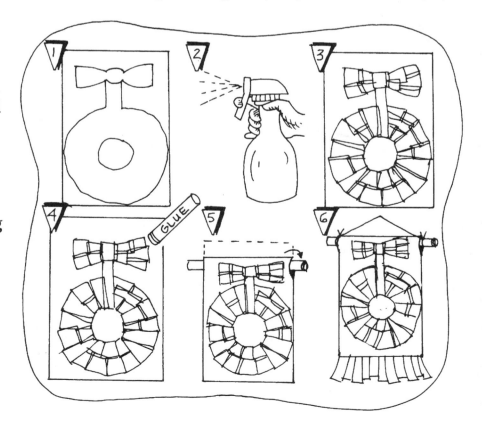

Ornaments and Other Decorations

"Happy Birthday, Jesus" Candle Holder

Younger Elementary Children

Make a tiny candle holder for a birthday candle that could be used to celebrate Jesus' birthday, then used again for family birthdays. If children made miniature individual Advent wreaths (see p. 9) for their rooms, then this candle holder can be put in the center of the wreath and the candle lit on Christmas Day.

What You Need

- Birthday candles
- Tempera paint and brushes
- Glitter (in a salt or spice shaker)
- White glue
- Old newspapers
- Cooked modeling clay

  Ingredients
  2 cups flour
  2 tablespoons oil
  2 cups water
  1 heaping tablespoon cream of tartar
  1 cup salt
  Electric skillet

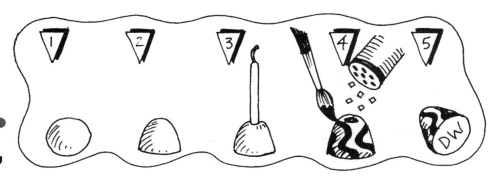

Combine all the ingredients for cooked modeling clay in a large electric skillet. Stir well and cook slowly until the dough begins to come together in a large ball. This will happen just as it is getting almost too hot to touch. Roll out on a board or smooth table and knead until cool enough for the children to handle. Give each child a small piece to knead and experiment with. The more the dough is handled, the better it becomes for molding. Store in an airtight plastic container. This recipe makes about two cups of dough.

What You Do

1. Cover your tables with old newspapers. Give each child a ball of dough about one and a half to two inches in diameter.

2. Tell children to flatten the ball on the bottom so it will stand firmly on its own, then fashion the little holder into any shape or style desired.

3. Give each child a birthday candle to push into the holder to form the hole. Then remove the candle and let dry.

4. The child can decorate the holder with tempera paint or glitter. Glitter may be applied by painting the holder with white glue, then sprinkling glitter on it from a salt or spice shaker. (Work over newspapers so you can gather the extra glitter easily and return it to the shaker.)

5. Put the child's initials on the bottom of the candle holder.

✳And More . . .

Add food coloring to make colored clay.

Baked Clay Christmas Ornaments

Younger and Older Elementary Children

What You Need

- Baked Clay

  Ingredients
    3/4 cup salt
    1 1/3 cups warm water
    4 cups flour
    Mixing bowl and spoon

- Cookie cutters, pencils, toothpicks, garlic press (optional)
- Ribbon
- Cookie sheet covered with aluminum foil
- Oven
- Markers or paint and brushes
- Paper punch
- Clear plastic spray or nail polish
- Water

What You Do

1. Let the children help mix the dough:
In the bowl, add the salt to the warm water and stir until the salt is dissolved.
- Add flour and mix well.
- Sprinkle a little flour on the work surface and knead the dough for about four minutes.

2. Tell the children to shape the dough with their fingers or use cookie cutters to cut out shapes. They can make faces or designs using a pencil, a toothpick, or other objects. Dough pressed through a garlic press makes hair. Tell them to moisten the dough with a little water before adding arms, legs, or decorations. They can use a pencil to sign and date the ornament on the back. Punch a hole in the top of the ornament for hanging.

3. Place the ornaments on a foil-covered cookie sheet and bake about twenty minutes at 300° to 350° F. Remove from oven as soon as the edges start to brown.

4. When ornaments are cool, let children paint them or use markers to color. Spray with clear plastic spray or coat with clear nail polish.

5. Tie a piece of ribbon through the hole for hanging.

String Ornaments

Older Elementary Children

What You Need

- String or colored embroidery floss
- Small round balloons
- White glue slightly diluted with water
- Shallow aluminum pan
- Scissors
- Waxed paper
- Ornament hangers (optional)

What You Do

1. Put the glue and water mixture in the pan.

2. Have each child slightly inflate a balloon.

3. Tell the children to dip a piece of colored embroidery floss or string into the diluted white glue, completely soaking the string and squeezing out the excess. Lengths of string about twelve inches long are easiest to work with.

4. Children can wind the string around the balloon in whatever pattern they prefer. They can add additional lengths of string as needed.

5. Place the balloons on waxed paper to dry. When string is stiff but not completely dry, have children carefully pop and remove the balloon.

6. Tie a loop of string to the top or attach an ornament hanger and suspend to complete drying.

In Our House . . . Ornament

Younger and Older Elementary Children

What You Need

- Poster board houses cut from pattern
- Colored fine-lined markers or pens
- Scraps of materials (paper, fabric, string, etc.)
- White glue
- Ornament hangers

What You Do

1. Ask children: "What is a Christmas family tradition in your house?" Tell them to write a few sentences describing that tradition on one side of the poster board house.

2. Tell children to decorate the other side of the poster board house to resemble their own house, using the markers and the scrap materials.

3. Attach an ornament hanger to the top of the house.

✸ And More . . .

Use tiny matchboxes with the matches removed to make three-dimensional houses. Children can write a few words describing the tradition, fold it up, and put it inside the matchbox.

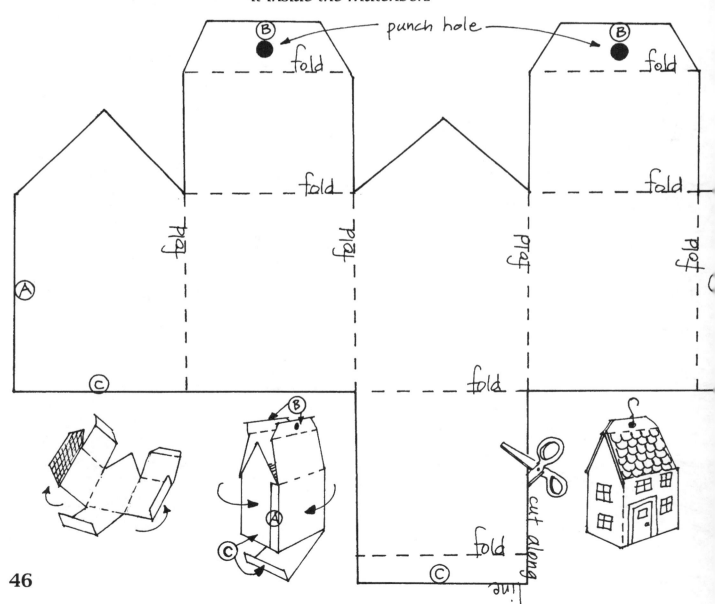

46

Poinsettias

Younger Elementary Children

What You Need for Each Child

- Red tissue paper cut into 4-inch squares (3 per flower)
- Green pipe cleaners
- Yellow craft beads
- 2-liter soda bottle caps
- Green construction paper
- Scissors and white glue
- 1-inch circles cut from black poster board

What You Do

1. Show the children how to place their four-inch squares of tissue paper on top of each other, rotating each additional square so that all twelve corners show.

2. Next, show the children how to attach a pipe cleaner around the outside rim of a soda bottle cap so that it looks like a lollipop.

3. Ask the children to put a little glue inside the bottle cap. Then tell them to place the center of the red squares over the bottle cap and use the cardboard circle to carefully push the tissue squares into the cap.

4. They can put several drops of glue on the black circle and adhere three or four yellow craft beads to it. Allow to dry.

5. Cut out leaves from green construction paper and glue to the pipe-cleaner stem.

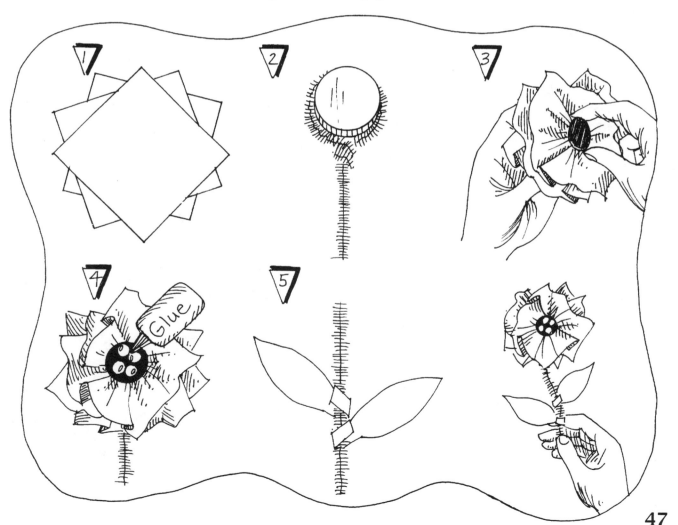

47

A Christmas Book

Older Elementary Children

This book makes a lovely table decoration for Christmas. Older elementary children can do all the work themselves, but carefully supervise the spray painting and the applying of the acrylic sealer.

What You Need

- Old copies of *Reader's Digest Condensed Books*, or books of similar size
- White glue
- Gold spray paint
- Paper doilies
- Old Christmas card pictures
- Mod Podge or other acrylic sealer
- Brushes
- Scissors
- 10-inch velvet ribbon
- Heavy plain beige or white stationery

What You Do

1. Open the book at the center and lay it flat. Have the children apply glue between the pages, except for the center pages, and along the sides. Let it dry. Put a weight on the book to flatten it as needed.

2. When it is completely dry, children can turn the book over and glue parts of paper doilies onto the outside to give it a hand-tooled leather look. Let it dry (use a hair dryer to shorten drying time).

3. Spray paint, or let the children spray paint the entire book gold. Let dry completely.

4. Children can trim Christmas card pictures to fit. They either glue pictures to both pages or carefully copy a Bible verse onto a sheet of heavy stationary and glue it to the facing page. Let dry.

5. Seal the book with the acrylic sealer and let dry.

6. Children can glue a velvet ribbon bookmark in place at the center top of the book.

Wrappings

● ● ● ● ● ● ● ● ● ● ● ●

Sponge Print Wrapping Paper

Young Children and Younger Elementary Children

What You Need

- Food coloring
- Small shallow dishes
- Clean sponges
- Patterns on p. 83
- Brown mailing paper or plain white shelf paper
- Scissors

What You Do

1. Cut the sponges into simple Christmas shapes using the patterns on p. 83.

2. For each color you will be using, put a few drops of water and four drops of a food coloring in a shallow dish.

3. Spread out the paper on a flat surface. Have the children dip a sponge into a color and press gently on the paper. Repeat to make a pattern.

4. Rinse out the sponge shapes thoroughly before changing colors; or use one shape per color.

5. Allow the wrapping paper to dry before using.

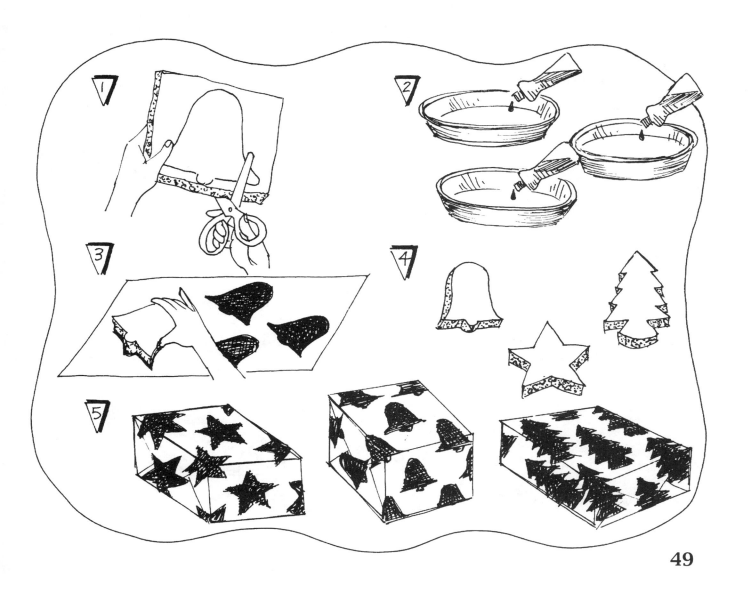

Marbleized Christmas Paper

Older Elementary Children

This wrapping paper is lovely for small gifts.

What You Need

- Small jars of model airplane paint, or other enamel (2 or 3 colors like red, green, and gold)
- Plastic spoons
- Sheets of heavy paper approximately 12" x 18"
- A dishpan or large flat pan
- Water
- Mineral spirits and old cloths for cleanup
- Sticks for stirring
- Old newspapers

What You Do

1. Fill the dishpan about two-thirds full of water.

2. Pour a little paint into a plastic spoon. Drip it slowly into the water. Repeat with the other two colors.

3. Let a child use the stir stick to swirl the different colors together just a little. Caution the child not to stir too much or the result will look muddy.

4. Have the child carefully lay the sheet of paper flat onto the water, leaving it in place for a few seconds.

5. Carefully peel the paper off the water. The paint will adhere to the paper in a beautiful marbleized pattern. Lay flat on newspapers to dry for several hours.

6. After two or three children have made marbleized paper, the water in the pan may need to be changed. Pour the used water into a large bucket and dispose of properly.

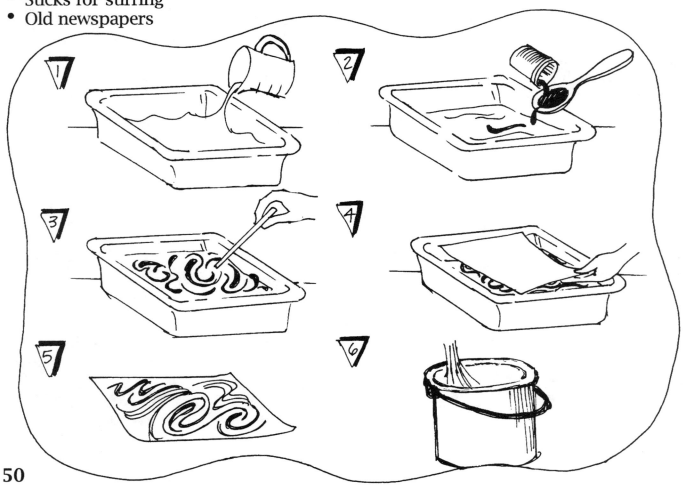

Bible Verse Paper

Younger Elementary Children

Here is a simple wrapping paper for children to make that can also help them remember parts of the Christmas story.

What You Need
- Brown mailing paper, or plain white wrapping paper
- Colored markers
- Scissors
- Rulers
- Pencils

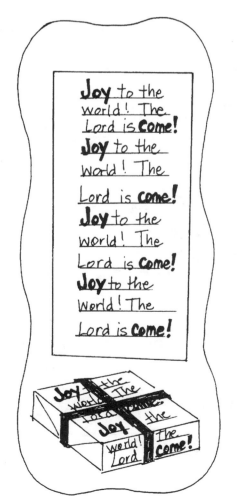

What You Do

1. In advance, print carefully in manuscript some short verses or phrases from verses from the Christmas stories in Luke and Matthew. Some examples:

And she gave birth to *her first born son*, and wrapped him in bands of cloth and laid him in a manger . . .

To you is born this day in the city of David *a Savior* who is *Christ the Lord* . . .

Glory to God in the highest, *and on earth peace* among those whom God favors . . .

Where is the child who has been born *king of the Jews?*

They offered him gifts of *gold, frankincense, and myrrh.*

You might also use phrases from familiar Christmas carols, like "Joy to the world! The Lord is come!"

2. Give each child a length of paper long enough to wrap a medium-sized package. Tell the children to make light pencil rules over the whole sheet of paper about one to two inches apart. Children can copy one of the phrases over and over lightly in pencil, until the entire sheet is filled.

3. Give the children two different colors of markers. Suggest that they use one color to print most of the words, and a contrasting color to print the italicized words.

✹And More . . .

—Make rebus wrapping paper. From sponges, cut a few simple shapes, such as a manger, a star, or an angel. Let the children copy phrases or verses that incorporate those words, leaving a space where the word appears. When they have finished covering the paper with words, they can dip the sponges in tempera paint and sponge print the missing word with the symbol.

—The children can choose certain words in the repeated phrase to embellish or decorate with markers, or make much larger than the other words (like JOY to the world!).

Handprint Wrapping Paper

Young Children

This activity is best done one on one with young children. Have other activities available and a helper to supervise the group as you help each child make the wrapping paper.

What You Need

- Newsprint or brown wrapping paper
- Red and green tempera paint (mixed with a little liquid dishwashing soap)
- Shallow aluminum pie pans
- Tub of water and towels for cleanup
- Paint smocks

What You Do

1. Arrange paint in pie pans.

2. Have the child put one hand flat in one color of paint and then make a handprint on the paper. Direct the child to continue making handprints with that hand in one color, leaving room on the paper for the other color.

3. Have the child rinse the messy hand in the tub of water and wipe it dry. Then the child can use the other hand to make palm prints of the other color.

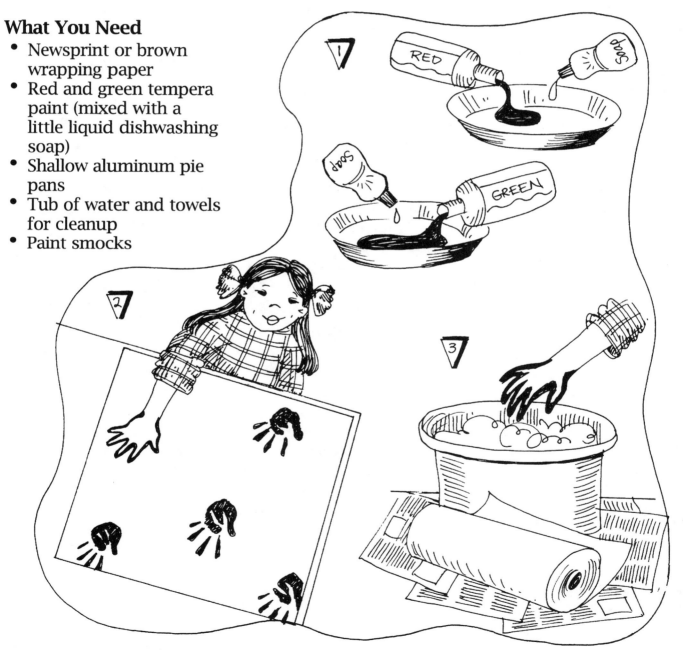

Christmas Trees

• • • • • • • • • • •

Tiny Live Evergreens

Younger and Older Elementary Children

Use small pinecones to make tiny trees for the village of Bethlehem, or larger pinecones to make miniature evergreens for presents.

What You Need
- Pinecones
- Grass seed
- Margarine tubs or other small containers to hold pinecones
- Bucket of water
- Modeling clay
- Scissors

What You Do

1. In advance, break off the stems of the pinecones so that they will stand upright by themselves. Soak the pinecones in the bucket of water for thirty minutes.

2. Tell the children to put a little modeling clay in the bottom of a margarine tub, sprinkle the pinecone thoroughly with grass seed, and stand up in the tub.

3. Put about a half inch of water in the bottom of each tub.

4. Place all the pinecones in a sunny window. In a few weeks the grass will begin to grow. Be sure the children check the pinecones frequently to be sure they have enough water.

5. When the grass is fairly long, children can clip it to form the shape of an evergreen tree.

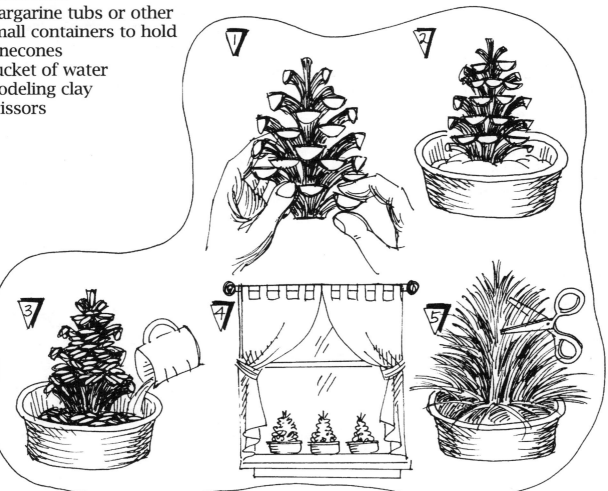

Two for the Price of One

Young Children

These two art projects demonstrate good stewardship of resources, while at the same time offering young children an intriguing alternative to painting with a paintbrush.

What You Need

- Green construction paper, 12" x 18"
- White construction paper, 12" x 18"
- Green tempera paint (add a little liquid dishwashing detergent)
- Small evergreen branches
- Scissors
- White glue and glue sticks
- Crayons and markers
- Bright scraps of construction and Christmas wrapping paper, bits of ribbon, etc., cut into small pieces
- (optional) Laminating equipment or clear self-adhesive shelf liner
- Pattern (p. 84)

Branch Painted Tree

What You Do

1. From the green construction paper, cut a Christmas tree frame using the pattern on p. 84. Try to cut the frame in one piece so that you have a tree-shaped frame and a tree-shaped piece of green paper.

2. Let children paint on white construction paper with the evergreen branches and green tempera paint. Set aside to dry.

3. When the paintings are dry, carefully glue a tree-shaped frame over each one. Allow the glue to dry completely.

Confetti Tree

What You Do

1. Let the children glue the small pieces of scrap materials on the green construction paper tree shapes to decorate them. They can also use crayons and markers. Allow the glue to dry.

2. If possible, laminate or cover with clear adhesive shelf liner to make more sturdy.

3-D Tissue Trees

Older and Younger Elementary Children

This project takes time to complete, but the results are well worth it.

What You Need

- Colored tissue in 1-inch squares (you will need several packages of green tissue paper, plus a variety of other bright colors)
- Poster board tree shapes, pattern, p. 84 (cut 2 from each sheet of poster board)
- White glue
- Pencils with erasers

What You Do

1. Show children how to place the eraser of the pencil in the center of the tissue square and pull the tissue up around the pencil eraser.

2. Have them dip the tissue square in glue, then place it on the tree shape and remove the pencil, leaving the tissue in place

3. Suggest that children cover most of the tree shape with green tissue, interspersing with colored tissue squares to make ornaments.

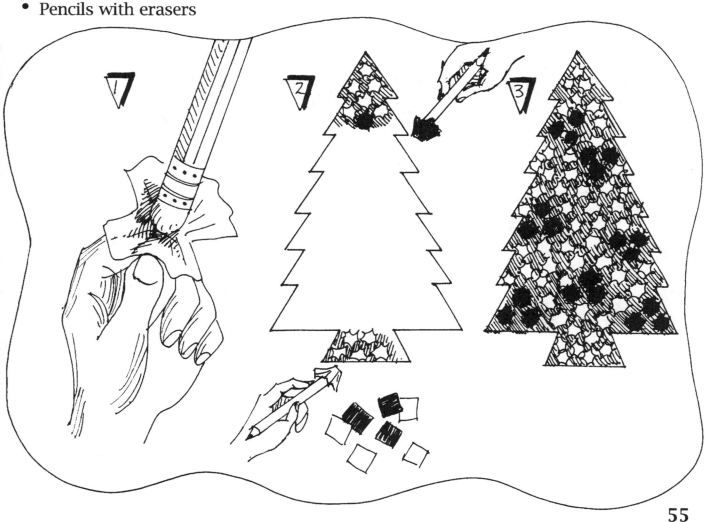

Squeeze-Bottle Glitter Trees

Young Children

What You Need

- Green poster board cut into a tree shape (cut 2 from each sheet of poster board)
- Mixture of equal parts of flour, water, and salt
- Plastic squeeze bottles (one for each color desired)
- Tempera paint (red, blue, yellow, silver, purple, gold)
- Newspapers
- Christmas tree pattern, p. 84

What You Do

1. In advance, prepare a squeeze bottle of each color you want to use. Make the flour-salt-water mixture, then add a little tempera paint.

2. Cover the table with newspaper. Give each child a Christmas tree shape. Let the children use the squeeze bottles to make interesting patterns on the cardboard.

3. Allow to dry completely.

✸ And More . . .

For young children the process of squeezing is more important than the product they produce. Let children enjoy using this technique on squares of cardboard just for fun.

Crèches and Manger Scenes

Stick Stables

Young Children

What You Need

- 12-inch square pieces of brown corrugated cardboard or brown wrapping paper
- Small straight twigs or sticks (6–8 per picture)
- White glue
- Crayons or markers
- Scissors
- Bits of straw (optional)
- Ruler

What You Do

1. In advance, prepare the stable shapes. Mark the center of each twelve-inch square, then measure four inches down each side. Make a straight line from the center point to the points on each side. Cut to make a stable-shaped piece.

2. Invite children to draw a picture of Mary, Joseph, and Jesus with crayons or markers.

3. With white glue, let them glue sticks on the sides and roof of the stable.

4. If they like, they can glue bits of straw to the floor of the stable.

5. Allow the glue to dry thoroughly before moving the pictures.

Cardboard Tube Créche

Children of All Ages

This créche is easy to make and can be handled safely by children of all ages. It can be an ongoing project over several weeks, or you could schedule one session to make the entire créche. Have older children make a créche for young children to use, or pair an older child with a young child to make a créche.

What You Need

- Cardboard bathroom tissue tubes or paper towel tubes
- Pipe cleaners cut in 2-inch lengths
- Brown or tan construction paper or white drawing paper and multicultural crayons
- Colored construction paper, wallpaper samples, fabric scraps, felt
- Black markers
- Rubber bands
- Yarn
- Glue sticks and white glue
- Donkey and sheep head patterns from p. 82 (photocopy)
- Cotton balls
- Scissors

What You Do

1. Make the créche figures. For each figure, children can glue a strip of tan or brown paper one inch wide around the top of the cardboard tube. This will be the face of the figure. They can use a black felt-tipped marker to make features on the face.

2. Tell children to glue a three-inch strip of construction paper around the bottom two-thirds of the cardboard tube.

3. To make arms, help children make a small hole in the tube just below the "head," put a dab of white glue on one end of a pipe cleaner, and insert it into the hole. Repeat on the opposite side.

4. Children can drape fabric scraps over the back and arms of the figure to make a robe. They can use a little white glue to secure the cloth. Then direct them to put fabric over the head of the figure and secure with a rubber band. They can cover the rubber band with yarn.

5. Children can vary the costume according to the figure being made. For example, striped fabric scraps or burlap would make good clothing for shepherds, and a pipe cleaner could be bent into a shepherd's crook. Scraps of brocade metallic fabric, or velvet or flocked wallpaper samples would be appropriate for the Wise Men.

6. To make the sheep, photocopy and cut out the pattern for the head. Children can glue it to the cardboard tube. They can twist two long pipe cleaners around the body for legs, or make holes in the bottom and insert four short pieces. Let them glue cotton balls on the tube to make the wool. Use the same procedure to make the donkey, but cover the body with brown paper or felt.

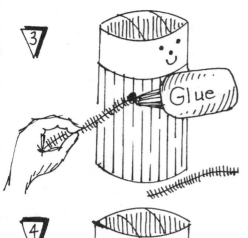

7. Make the stable. Have children paint the larger box with brown tempera paint. Allow to dry thoroughly. Glue on sticks to make a roof. Have children dilute white glue with a little water and paint on the stable floor, then adhere the straw to the glue. Paint the small box for a manger and glue in straw.

8. To make the Jesus figure, have children make features with a black marking pen on a wooden clothespin. Children can pad the clothespin with several cotton balls and wrap in a scrap of lightweight fabric. Secure by wrapping with yarn.

✳ And More . . . .

In some Latin American countries, people make the village of Bethlehem as well as the crèche. Moravians have a similar custom in creating a putz. Gather boxes of various sizes and scrap materials of all kinds. Using pictures of houses in biblical times as a guide, children can recreate Bethlehem. Have some children make crèche figures and others to make other people and animal figures for the town. Remind the children that Bethlehem was very crowded!

For stable:
- Small cardboard box (use completed crèche figures to gauge a good size)
- Brown tempera paint and brushes
- Small sticks or twigs, straw
- Jewelry box (for manger)
- Cotton balls
- White glue
- Straw
- Clothespins
- Fabric scraps
- Yarn

Shoebox Triptych Créche

Older Elementary Children

A triptych is a three-sided piece of art. Artisans in El Salvador make beautiful triptychs and wall plaques by carving and painting wood panels.

What You Need for Each Créche

- A shoebox with a lid
- White drawing paper cut to fit inside the bottom of the box, inside both ends of the box, and a piece slightly smaller than the two lid halves
- Additional sheets or scraps of white drawing paper
- Tempera paint (red, blue, green) and brushes
- Colored markers
- White glue
- Scissors
- Colored plastic tape

What You Do

1. Have the children use sharp scissors to cut off the sides of the shoebox top and then to cut the top in half.

2. Children can use one color to paint the outside of the shoebox and both sides of the top. Set aside to dry. When the two halves of the top are dry, they can cover the edges with colored plastic tape.

3. On the sheet of paper cut to fit inside the bottom of the box, have children use markers to draw the stable, Mary, and Joseph. On the sheets cut to fit the ends, have them draw nativity animals. On the sheets slightly smaller than the half-lid pieces, have them draw shepherds.

4. On a separate scrap of white paper, children can draw Jesus in the manger. They should cut out this piece, adding a tab across the bottom and folding it under.

5. Children can assemble the créches by gluing in the sheets of paper and the stand-up manger piece. They can attach the side pieces of the triptych with colored plastic tape.

6. If they like, they can cut decorations from scraps of construction paper to glue to the outside of the box, or add painted embellishments.

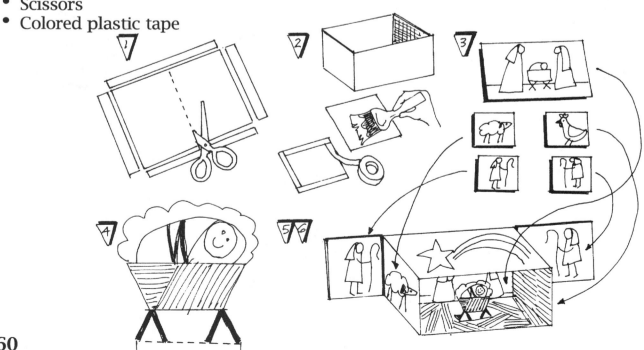

Woodland Créche Candle Holder

Older Elementary Children

This créche requires some advance work by someone with very basic woodworking skills. Some older elementary children can handle this task. Constructing the créche takes time, but the results are well worth it.

What You Need

- 8-inch long sections of logs, approximately 6" in diameter, with a 3/4-inch hole drilled approximately 1" deep
- 6-inch candles
- Sweet gum balls
- 1/2-inch natural finish wooden beads
- Nails
- 3–4 hammers (depending on how many children will be using them)
- Natural materials (acorn caps, small stones, moss, twigs, pieces of bark, seed pods, small pinecones, etc.)
- Heavy sisal twine or string
- Natural burlap
- Colored miniature straw flowers (available at craft stores)

What You Do

1. Show the children how to put a wooden bead on top of a sweet gum ball and hammer a nail through the hole in the bead, through the sweet gum ball and into the log (some children may need help doing this). They can make figures for Mary and Joseph.

2. Let children use the natural materials and their imaginations to complete the créche. A small seed pod or bark piece filled with moss would make a good manger. Show them how to unravel the twine to make hair to glue on. Top with small pieces of burlap for headgear.

3. Small twigs, stones, straw flowers, and other materials can be used to decorate the surface créche.

4. Complete by inserting the candle in the hole.

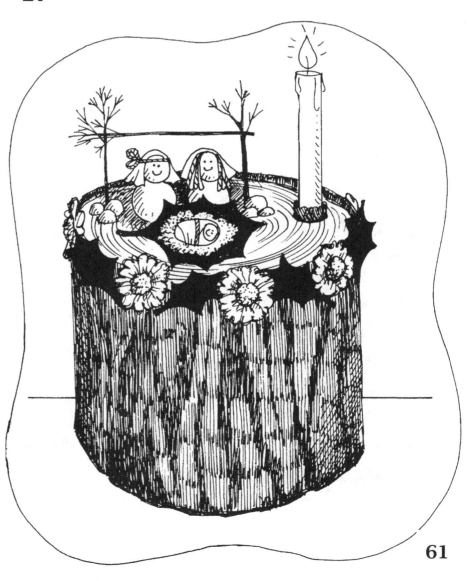

Things to Do
● ● ● ● ● ● ● ● ● ● ● ● ●
Posada Journey

Children of All Ages

What You Need

- Figures of Mary and Joseph (créche scene figures, or Giant Broom Puppets, see p. 67)
- Biblical dress-ups (for younger children)
- Party food, piñata, decorations

What You Do

1. In advance, recruit older children, youth, or adults to be inside the places where the group stops. This could be rooms along a hallway, locations in a larger room, or actual houses.

   Tell the children that the custom of Las Posadas originated in Spanish-speaking countries. Posada means "inn" or "lodging." On each of the nine days before Christmas, a group of people reenact the journey of Mary and Joseph seeking shelter in Bethlehem. They go to a home and sing a song requesting that they be allowed to enter. The people inside the house sing back, denying entrance. Finally at the last house the people inside sing that they can enter and find shelter. Everyone celebrates with food, games, and music, and often a piñata is broken.

2. Let children who want to dress up in biblical dress-ups. Have two children at the front of the group carry the figures of Mary and Joseph.

3. Sing through the song. The following is a simple song that can be used to the tune of "I Saw Three Kings."

   > Good innkeeper, may we come in
   >   May we come in, May we come in,
   > Good innkeeper, may we come in
   >   May we come in and find shelter?
   >
   > *(Response)*
   >   No traveller, you can't come in
   >   You can't come in, you can't come in.
   >   No traveller, you can't come in
   >   You can't come in and find shelter.
   >
   > *(Final response)*
   >   Yes, traveler, you can come in,
   >   You can come in, you can come in,
   >   Yes, traveler, you can come in,
   >   You can come in and find shelter.

   —Adapted from a song by Marilyn Aberle

4. End your posada in a large room where there can be a celebration.

A Journey to Bethlehem
Young Children

What You Do

1. Use this action poem:

(Begin walking in place)
How many days to Bethlehem—
From Nazareth to David's town?
Joseph and Mary walked all the way,
Up dusty rocky roads and down.
They must have camped along the road;
I wonder what they took to eat?
No doubt they were glad to get there at last,
To take off their sandals and rest their feet.
(Sit down quickly to rest feet)

2. Say to the children:

Let's walk like Joseph when he started out on their trip. Maybe he started out walking fast. Lots of other people also had to go to their hometowns and register. Let's wave to the people we know along the way!

(Walk in place at a good pace and wave to imaginary people as you repeat the poem again.)

Now let's walk like Mary. She was going to have a baby soon, so she isn't walking as fast as Joseph.

(Walk in place slowly as you repeat the poem.)

It took Mary and Joseph several days to reach Bethlehem since they had to walk all the way. By the time they reached Bethlehem, they must have been very tired. Let's walk like Mary and Joseph as they come into Bethlehem.

(Repeat the poem very slowly as you walk in place. Encourage the children to drag their feet and to take slow, heavy steps).

Whose Story?

Older Elementary Children

This activity helps older elementary children understand the two accounts of the Christmas story found in the Gospels of Matthew and Luke.

What You Need
- Bibles
- 2 posters or sheets of newsprint, labeled "Matthew's Good News Paper" and "Luke's Good News Paper"
- Tape
- Story cards with the facts printed on the right side of the page.

Joseph has a dream and an angel speaks to him.

An angel visits Zechariah with news.

Wise Men come from the east seeking Jesus.

An angel brings news to Mary.

Mary visits her cousin Elizabeth.

The Wise Men ask Herod where to find the king of the Jews.

John the Baptist is born.

The Wise Men follow the star and find the child in the house with his mother.

Mary and Joseph journey to Bethlehem to be registered for the census.

The Wise Men give gifts of gold, frankincense, and myrrh.

There is no room for them in the inn, and Jesus is born in a stable.

The shepherds get joyous news from heavenly visitors. They visit the baby.

(You can add other facts from Matthew, like the flight to Egypt, if you like.)

What You Do

1. Tell the children that Matthew and Luke each are writing a Good News Paper, and each one has a different story to tell about the birth of Jesus.

2. Let the children use the Bibles to help them sort out the story cards to tape on either the Luke or Matthew story sheet.

3. Compare the two stories. Why do the children think the accounts are different?

All Together in Bethlehem

Young Children

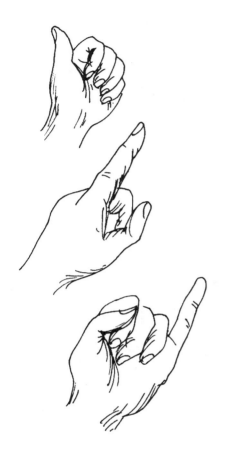

What You Do

1. Use the following as a fingerplay:

Here is Joseph. He named Jesus.
(*hold up thumb*)

Here is Mary. She was Jesus' mother.
(*hold up forefinger*)

Here is Jesus, a very special baby.
(*hold up little finger*)

Here are the shepherds. They came to see the baby.
(*hold up middle fingers so all fingers are up*)

All together in Bethlehem.
(*clap hands*)

2. Use the poem as you gather the children around the créche. Ask someone to find Joseph and hold the figure up. Say the first line of the fingerplay. Then ask another child to find Mary and hold the figure up. Say the second line of the fingerplay. Continue until the children are holding all the figures, adding the following line if you have the appropriate figures:

"Here are the animals. They watched over Jesus."

Finish with the last line. Then repeat the fingerplay again, this time asking the children to hold up their figure when they hear the appropriate line.

EPIPHANY

. . . signifies the manifestation of God among us in human form.

It is a time to *return* . . .

Replacing the evergreens and lights of Christmas with the clean-swept order of our day-to-day lives.

It is a time to *reflect* . . .

Considering the ministry on earth of the adult born as a baby in a manger.

It is a time to *proclaim* . . .

Sharing with each other and with others the good news of God's revelation in Christ.

It is a time to *expand* . . .

Broadening our vision to include people of all races and cultures and times.

Images of the Magi

●　●　●　●　●　●　●　●　●　●

On January 6, Three Kings' Day is a major celebration in Puerto Rico. Children dress up as the three kings and parade through the streets. Images of the three kings are a part of parades and processions in many cultures on this day.

Giant Broom Puppets

Younger and Older Elementary Children

What You Need

For each puppet:
- Standard broom (preferably new) with a smooth handle
- Large grocery bag
- Old newspapers
- Heavyweight rubber band and heavy string
- Screwdriver or other blunt tool
- Small cardboard carton or shoebox with lid taped on securely
- Costume items such as colorful shirt, blouse, or old bathrobe
- Scarves or lengths of fabric for headdresses
- Yarn, buttons, felt, colored markers, construction-paper scraps, gold or silver foil, etc.
- Poster board
- White glue
- Scissors

What You Do

1. To make the puppet head, help the child fill the grocery bag loosely with crumpled newspaper. Place filled bag over the head of the broom, fitting bristles into the middle of the bag. Gather the bag opening snugly around the broomstick and fasten tightly with string.

2. To make shoulders, use the screwdriver to punch a hole in the top and bottom of the carton or shoebox large enough for the broomstick to go through. The hole should be small enough for the broomstick to be a tight fit. Slide the box up the broomstick until it is just under the bag and wind a heavy rubber band around the stick just under the carton to keep it from slipping.

3. Children can use felt, construction-paper scraps, markers, and buttons to form facial features on the bag. Yarn can be used to make beards and hair.

4. Let the children "dress" the puppet with the costume items and fabric you have available. Make crowns with poster board and cover with foil or decorate with sequins or buttons.

5. A child can walk behind the Wise Man puppet carrying it in front or carry it to the side.

✳And More . . .

Make an entire Nativity scene of giant puppets, including Mary, Joseph, the shepherds, and an angel or two.

Paper Plate Puppet Faces

Younger and Older Elementary Children

These puppets can be held aloft and carried in a Three Kings' procession.

What You Need

- Heavy paper plates (shiny surfaced red, brown, black, and yellow or white)
- Construction-paper scraps (blue, brown, white, red)
- White glue
- Yarn (brown or black)
- Silver or gold poster board, or cardboard and silver and gold paint
- Fabric remnants (brocade, velvet, lamé, or other rich-looking materials)
- Scrap materials (doilies, buttons, rickrack, and so forth)
- Thin dowel sticks
- Masking tape, stapler, sharp scissors, felt-tipped markers
- Pencils
- Sharp scissors

What You Do

1. Have children use pencils to lightly sketch a face on the paper plate. Then have them use sharp scissors to cut out eyes and around the bottom and sides of the nose, leaving the top of the nose attached. They can push out slightly on the nose so that it is three-dimensional. They can use construction paper and other scraps to add details to the faces.

2. Have children glue yarn to the top of the face to make hair. They can then choose a fabric remnant to staple to the top of the plate so that it hangs down behind the plate.

3. Using one of the patterns on pp. 86–87, children can make a crown from poster board or cardboard and use scrap materials to decorate. Have them slide the crown slightly down over the plate and the fabric.

4. Have children tape a dowel stick securely to the back of the plate.

✱And More . . .

Children can tie curled ribbons or metallic star garlands to the dowel sticks.

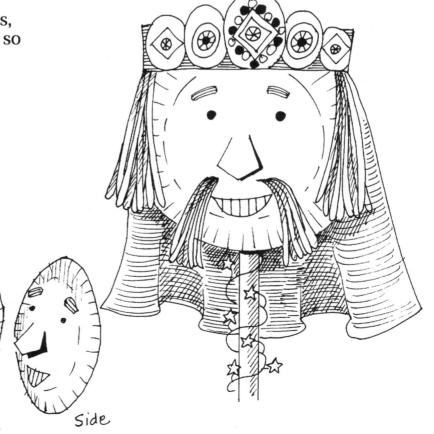

back

side

68

Night Visitor Pictures

Children of All Ages

This technique results in a dramatic picture of night-time scenes such as the journey and the visit of the Wise Men. Young children will focus mostly on the technique and the satisfyingly rich colors, while elementary children will appreciate what the technique brings to the subject matter.

What You Need

- Flat baking pan or dishpan containing water to a depth of about an inch
- Dark blue or black construction paper (large sheets work best)
- White and colored chalk
- Old newspapers
- Hair spray
- Damp cloths for hands

What You Do

1. Cover the work area with several layers of newspapers.

2. Tell the children to dip a piece of construction paper into the water, wetting it thoroughly.

3. Next children draw a picture on the wet paper with the colored chalk. The chalk will make smooth strokes and the colors will be rich and deep, similar to paint.

4. Lay the finished pictures on dry newspapers. A light coating of hair spray when the picture is completely dry will help to "fix" the chalk so it will not rub off.

✸ And More . . .

Use this technique for portraying the angels' appearance to the shepherds, Nativity scenes, or the flight into Egypt.

3-D Three Kings

Young Children and Younger Elementary Children

What You Need

- 12" x 18" white drawing paper (6 sheets per child)
- Crayons and markers
- Stapler
- Old newspapers
- Scissors

What You Do

1. Tell the children to draw one of the three kings on each of the three sheets of paper. Encourage them to make the figure take up the entire page.

2. When the drawings are done, show the children how to draw a rough outline around the figure. (Don't try to outline any small parts, just get the general shape.) Children cut out the figures, or you can cut them out.

3. Children can trace the outlines of the figures on additional sheets of paper and cut them out. Put the second sheet back to back with the cutout figure and staple on three sides.

4. Stuff figures lightly with wadded-up newspaper, then staple shut the final opening.

✷And More . . .

Make an entire crèche set of three-dimensional figures. Let each child make one figure and display the finished figures together.

Crowns

Paper Bag Crowns

Young Children

What You Need
- #12 paper grocery bags
- Bright construction-paper scraps
- White glue

What You Do

1. Let each child try on a grocery bag. Help them to fold back the open edge several times to make it sturdier.

2. Children can cut or tear paper scraps to make jewels and glue them on to decorate the crowns.

✸And More . . .

—Older children will enjoy gluing bits of metallic rickrack, large sequins, old buttons, cut pieces of silver or gold doilies, or other beautiful decorations to their crowns. Allow to dry thoroughly before wearing.
—Try decorating using the three-dimensional tissue method.

Poster Board Crowns

Older Elementary Children

Matthew's Gospel does not tell us how many magi there were. Perhaps there were many more than three! All the children in your group can make crowns and process.

What You Need
- 2 colors of poster board (white, silver, gold, black, blue, red)
- Crown patterns from pp. 86–87
- Sharp scissors
- Tape or stapler
- White glue

What You Do

1. Enlarge the crown patterns according to the instructions. Trace onto poster board and cut out two or three templates.

2. Have children cut out a crown from poster board, saving their scraps.

3. Have children trade their scraps with a child who has a different color poster board.

4. Tell children to use their scissors to make cutout places in their crowns, and to cut scraps of the contrasting color into small diamonds, hearts, circles, or other shapes. These shapes can be glued to the crown to decorate it. Encourage children to layer shapes, for instance, to cut diamonds in three sizes and stack them up as a decoration.

5. Connect ends of the crown with tape or staples.

✸And More . . .

Children can add remnants of brocades, velvets, or satins to their crowns. Material can either be stapled to the inside back of the crown so that it hangs down the back, or it can be stapled all around the inside of the crown so that it puffs up.

Stars and Other Symbols of Light

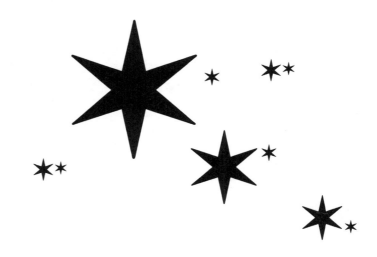

Light is a powerful symbol of Epiphany. It represents God's manifestation as Jesus, the Light of the World. The star that led the Wise Men to the child Jesus is the central image of Epiphany.

Shiny Stars

Young Children and Younger Elementary Children

What You Need

- Star frames cut from 8 1/2" x 11" construction paper (see "Two for the Price of One" on p. 54 for directions for cutting frame)
- Pieces of clear self-adhesive shelf liner, 11" x 17"
- Scraps of used shiny or foil Christmas wrapping paper, torn into small pieces

What You Do

1. In advance, tape a piece of shelf liner sticky side out to the table in front of where each child will work. Carefully peel the backing from half of the length of the liner. Adhere the star frame over the liner.

2. Let the children fill up the inside of the frame with small pieces of wrapping paper and foil.

3. When the inside is completely filled, carefully peel the backing from the other half and fold over to seal.

Aluminum Foil Star

Older Elementary Children

What You Need

- Two 8-inch squares of heavy aluminum foil
- One 8-inch square of cardboard for each star
- Star pattern (p. 85), traced and cut out
- Old newspapers
- Scissors
- Pencils with dull points
- Colored marking pens
- Rubber cement
- Darning needle and thread
- Ornament hangers

What You Do

1. Tell the children to fold their newspaper in half to make a thick pad. Next the children lay one piece of foil on the pad, shiny side down. Then place the pattern on the foil. Next they should trace the star design with a dull pencil. (A sharp pencil will poke a hole in the foil.) Have them turn the foil over. There will be a raised star pattern on the shiny side. Follow the same procedure with the other piece of foil.

2. Direct the children to color their stars on the shiny side with marking pens.

3. Next the children should brush rubber cement on the dull side of each foil square and on one side of the cardboard square and let them dry. They then lay one of the foil squares shiny side up on the cardboard and smooth it in place, being careful not to press down on the raised design. Tell the children to cut out this star.

4. Have them brush rubber cement on the cardboard side of the star and let it dry. Next they cut out the other foil star, lay it on the cardboard, and press it in place.

5. To hang the star, stitch a thread through one point of the star to make a loop. Tie a knot to fasten it to an ornament hanger.

● ●

Crayon Shaving Stars

Younger and Older Elementary Children

Melted crayon shavings make luminous stars.

What You Need

- Pieces of waxed paper, 8 1/2" x 11", 2 for each child
- Small pencil sharpeners
- Star-shaped frames, cut from 8 1/2" x 11" construction paper (see p. 54 for directions)
- Stapler
- Iron

What You Do

1. Give each child a piece of waxed paper, a small pencil sharpener, and an assortment of gold, pink, yellow, silver, and orange crayons.

2. Tell the children to use the pencil sharpener to make crayon shavings to cover the waxed paper.

3. When the children are done, put the second piece of waxed paper on top. Using the iron on lowest setting, carefully melt the designs. (Supervise carefully.)

4. Staple the star frames to the children's designs.

Luminaries

Older Elementary Children

Luminaries were first used in Mexico. Now they can be found all over the southwest and in Florida at Christmastime. Luminaries can be used to line and illumine a sidewalk leading up to the entrance of a home or church. Have someone watching the luminaries at all times to be sure none catch fire, and have available a bucket of water just in case.

What You Need

- Paper lunch sacks
- Patterns of symbols on p. 83
- White or yellow tissue paper cut into 6-inch squares
- Glue sticks
- Sharp scissors
- Sand
- Utility or votive candles

What You Do

1. Have the children trace one of the symbols on both sides of the paper sack about two inches up from the bottom. Simple shapes work best.

2. Tell the children to use the point of the scissors to carefully make a hole along the outline of the pattern, and to cut out the shape. They can do the same on the other side.

3. Direct the children to open the lunch bag and stand it up. On the inside of the bag on both sides, have them go around the outline of the cutout shape with a glue stick, and carefully glue the tissue paper square over the opening.

4. When the glue is dry, children can fill the bags with an inch or two of sand and stand the candle up inside the bag.

Tin Can Lanterns

Older Elementary Children

What You Need

- Soup cans with labels removed
- Water
- Freezer compartment of a refrigerator
- Hammers
- Large nails
- Paper cut to fit around the cans
- Tape
- Pencils
- Glossy black spray paint (or red, green, or purple)
- Votive candles

What You Do

1. In advance, fill the cans with water and freeze until solid.

2. Have children draw a simple design on the paper (something they can render by punching holes, such as stars, crosses, a dove, etc.).

3. Have them tape the design to the outside of the cans.

4. Following the lines of the design, have them use the hammer to drive the nail into the can. The more holes they make, the more light will shine from their lanterns.

5. Have them remove the paper from the outside of the can. Run the cans under hot water to melt the ice, and dispose of it.

6. Dry the cans and spray paint the outside. Allow to dry.

7. Put a votive candle inside each can.

✳ And More . . .

Use coffee cans of various sizes sprayed with matte black paint.

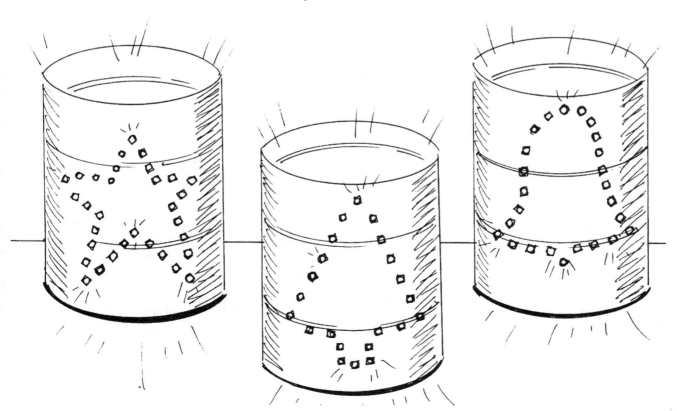

Gifts and Things to Share

● ● ● ● ● ● ● ● ● ● ● ● ●

Epiphany Cake

Children of All Ages

In France and in Puerto Rico, a Three Kings' Cake is made to celebrate Epiphany. Whoever finds a bean in a portion of the cake is designated king or queen for the day.

What You Need

- *Ingredients for cake:*
    1 cup brown sugar
    1/3 cup shortening
    1/2 teaspoon nutmeg
    2 teaspoons cinnamon
    1 1/4 cups water
    1 cup raisins
    1/2 teaspoon ground
        cloves
    1 teaspoon soda
    1 teaspoon salt
    2 teaspoons water
    2 cups flour
    1 teaspoon baking
        powder
    3 or more dried beans,
        wrapped in foil
- Canned vanilla butter
  creme frosting
- Colored gumdrops
- Large saucepan
- Measuring spoons, cups
- Sifter and spoon
- Round cake pan
- Oven

What You Do

1. Tell the children to put the first seven ingredients in a saucepan and boil for three minutes.
2. They then add the teaspoons of soda and salt and the two teaspoons of water.
3. Have the children sift and blend in the flour and baking powder.
4. When the batter is mixed, have them add the beans.
5. Bake at 325° F for about one hour.
6. When the cake is cool, the children can frost it with canned frosting and decorate with colored gumdrops to represent the jewels on the kings' crowns.

A Gift of Commitment

Older Elementary Children

What You Need

- Small gift boxes (like jewelry boxes)
- Wrapping paper
- Ribbons
- Tape
- Fine-lined markers or pens
- Scissors

What You Do

1. Remind the children that the Wise Men brought gifts to give to the child Jesus. These were valuable gifts, meant to honor a king. Begin a discussion by asking the children, What kind of gifts can we give to honor Jesus? Talk about how acts of service to the church, to parents, or to those who need assistance in some way (like young parents who need babysitters or older people who might need help with yard work) are gifts worthy of the Christ-child.

2. Ask each child to think about a gift of service that he or she can offer someone. Tell the children to be sure to offer something that they will really do. Let children write down the gift of service and the name of the recipient on a sheet of paper.

3. Give children small boxes, wrapping paper, scissors, ribbon, and tape. Tell them to wrap the top and the bottom of the box separately so that the box can be opened.

4. Once the boxes are wrapped, tell the children to fold up the sheet of paper on which they have written the gifts of service and put them inside the boxes.

5. Stack the completed boxes where they can serve as a reminder to the children of their commitments. Or let children take them home and ask that they keep the boxes in their bedrooms to remind them of what they wrote.

Take flowers to a sick friend.

Evergreen Potpourri Sachets

Young Children and Younger Elementary Children

Tradition has it that the evergreens used for decorating during the Christmas season have been transformed into something beyond the ordinary. In some cultures, part of the evergreen decoration—a branch from the tree or a sprig of mistletoe—is set aside and saved.

What You Need

- Evergreen needles chopped fine (Balsam and spruce work the best.)
- Other potpourri ingredients such as dried flower petals and spices (Packaged potpourri can be purchased at a craft store.)
- 5-inch squares of red or green nylon netting
- Rubber bands
- Narrow red or green satin ribbon
- Gift tags
- Scissors

What You Do

1. Give each child a square of nylon netting. Have children place a small amount of each potpourri ingredient in the center of the square. Give children the opportunity to smell each ingredient. Tell them that two of the gifts that the Wise Men brought Jesus were incense and an ointment with a strong fragrance.

2. Tell children to pull up the four corners of the netting to make a ball and secure with a rubber band.

3. Children can tie ribbon around the potpourri sachets to hide the rubber band and attach a small gift tag.

✳ And More . . .

—*Instead of making sachets, children can fill small decorated gift boxes with the potpourri.*
—*Use metallic star garland to tie around the sachets in place of the ribbon.*

Things to Do
• • • • • • • • • • •
To Nazareth

Young Children

What You Need
• Snack foods to share (figs, olives, bread, cheese)

What You Do

1. Say this poem for the children:

How many days to Nazareth—
>From distant lands, by the light of a star.
>>The Wise Men journeyed all the way.
>They must have camped along the road,
>>I wonder what they had to eat!
>They must have been glad when they
>>found the child,
>And laid their presents at his feet.

2. To begin a discussion about the Wise Men, ask the children, When do you think the kings had to travel?

If no one is sure, remind them that the kings were following the star, so they would have to travel at night when the star was visible. Tell the children that the kings came from far away. It may have been a long time before they found the child.

3. Share together some foods the Wise Men might have carried with them to eat, like cheese, bread, figs, and olives. Repeat the poem again for the children.

A Long Journey

Young Children and Younger Elementary Children

What You Do

Use this action story to help children "live into" the account of the Wise Men's journey.

My friends and I look up into the skies every night. *(look off into the distance, with hands shading eyes)* We are looking for a new and bright star that will tell us a new king has been born. Some nights we stay up very late and get very sleepy *(yawn)*. Finally, one night we do see a star *(shout "Hurray!")*.

The next day, we begin to get ready for a very long trip to find the baby. We must travel on camels. We pack our bags *(pretend to put things in bag)*. We must travel at night because we cannot see the star in the daytime. So we go to bed when we are usually having lunch *(close eyes, rest head on hands)*.

Then we wake up *(stretch)*, and get up on our camels *(reach way up)*.

We ride up hills and down hills *(slap knees to make hoof sounds)*.

We go through tall grasses *(rub palms together to make swishing noises)*.

After many, many days we come to a house where the star has led us *(point up as if to a star)*.

Here is Mary, and here is little Jesus *(kneel down)*. We put our presents down for the very special child *(pretend to put gifts down)*.

● ●

Gifts of Hay

Older Elementary Children

What You Need

• Large basket or decorated carton filled with hay

What You Do

1. Explain to the children that in Puerto Rico, Three Kings' Day is the time when gifts are received. Instead of having a Christmas tree, children gather grasses or hay and put it under their beds or on the roofs for the camels of the Three Kings.

2. Your group can celebrate Three Kings' Day by choosing a recipient for gifts, such as a food pantry or a homeless shelter, and the gifts you will try to supply. For instance, a homeless shelter might need personal care items such as disposable razors, toothbrushes, or soap, while a food pantry might need to replace staple foods depleted by the holiday season.

3. Have children bring in the items your group has chosen. For every item received, remove some hay until all the hay is replaced by gifts.

PATTERNS

Jesse Tree Symbols

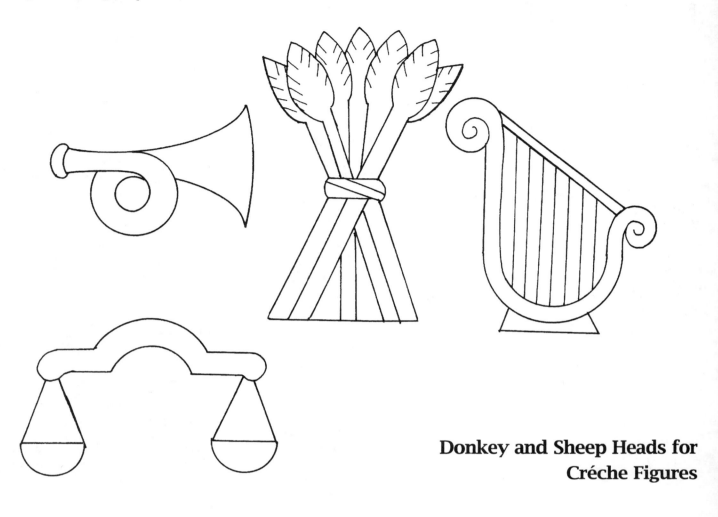

Donkey and Sheep Heads for Créche Figures

83

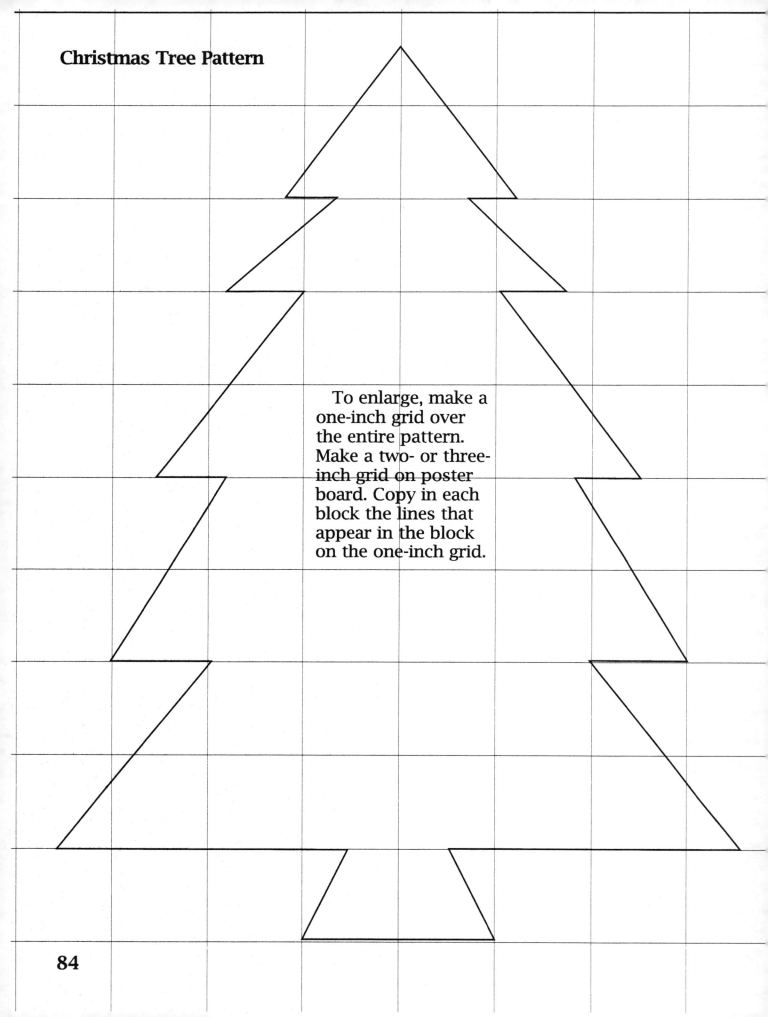

Christmas Tree Pattern

To enlarge, make a one-inch grid over the entire pattern. Make a two- or three-inch grid on poster board. Copy in each block the lines that appear in the block on the one-inch grid.

84

Star Frame Pattern

Crown Pattern

Extend both ends of the
crown six to eight inches.

Crown Pattern

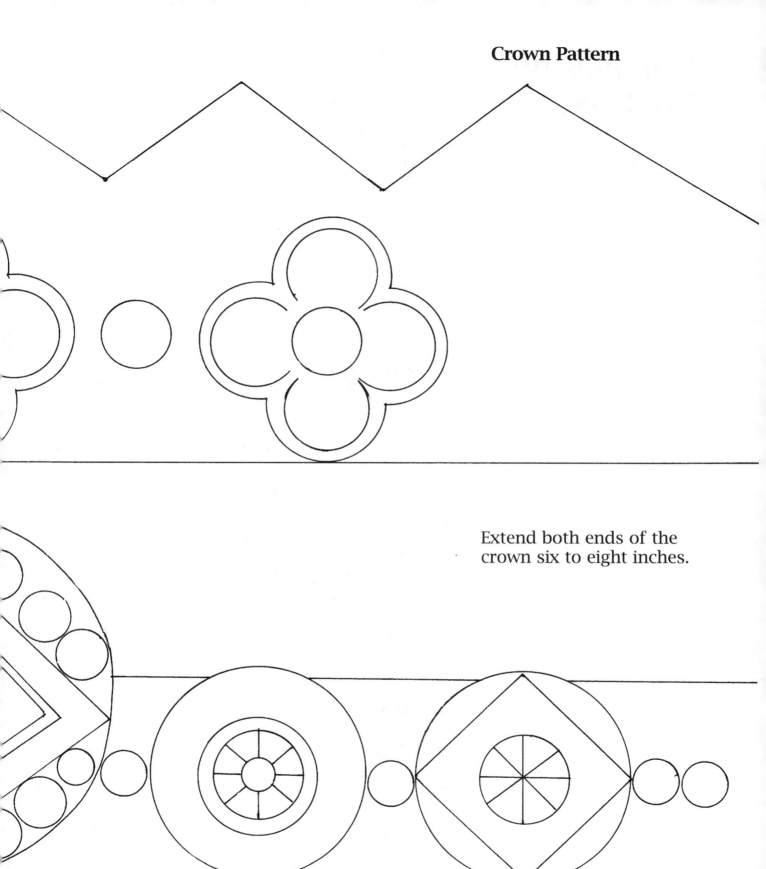

Extend both ends of the
crown six to eight inches.

87

Activities by Age Groups
●●●●●●●●●●●

Older Elementary Children

Children of All Ages

Index
●　●　●　●　●　●　●　●　●　●　●　●　●